RUSSIAN PORTRAITS

by
CLARE SHERIDAN

Edited by
MARK ALMOND

*Lecturer in Modern History,
Oriel College, Oxford*

947
.0854

Ian Faulkner Publishing
Cambridge · England

Ian Faulkner Publishing Ltd
Lincoln House
347 Cherry Hinton Road
Cambridge CB1 4DJ

First published 1921
by Jonathan Cape

A CIP record for this book is available from the British
Library.

ISBN 1-85763-004-1

Printed in Great Britain by Billings and Sons Ltd

CONTENTS

INTRODUCTION

by Mark Almond

The story in this book reads a little like a fairy-tale. A war-widowed heiress with a gift for sculpture happens to fall in with foreign revolutionaries on a secret mission to her country. They recognise her talent and invite her back to the very centre of the new power in order to immortalise its leaders through her art. She penetrates to the inner sanctum of a conspiracy dedicated to overthrowing everything to which she has been accustomed so far and survives to tell the tale. All that is lacking is romance to complete the story.

Few would have predicted Clare[1] Sheridan's later career as an artist and writer when she was born in September 1885. She was the product of one of the many late-nineteenth-century marriages between English family and American money, like her cousin Winston Churchill or his rival Neville Chamberlain. Her father, Moreton Frewen, was a country gentleman and adventurer. Her mother, Clara, was the sister of Jennie Jerome, Lady Randolph Churchill. She was brought up

---

1 She cut out the original 'i' as an adult.

to be socially adept and was fluent in French and German, but her formal education was neglected. The life of a débutante held little appeal for her and she was glad to take up with William (Wilfred) Sheridan, a stockbroker, who was amused by her ignorance of his great-great-grandfather, Richard Brinsley Sheridan, and encouraged her to read widely in English literature. She made several early efforts at fiction, but her real gifts seemed to lie in sketching and sculpting. Only later were her skills as a descriptive writer and memoirist discovered.

Her married life was marked by tragedy. Less than four years after marrying Wilfred Sheridan in 1910, her daughter Elizabeth died. Clare modelled an angel for her daughter's tomb and discovered her true vocation. She preferred to be called a 'sculptor', the first sign of her later liberation from woman's conventional role. In 1915 Wilfred was killed on the Western Front, leaving her with a new-born son, Richard, whom his father had never seen.

Her personal bereavement, as well as the universal carnage of the First World War, moved Clare Sheridan deeply and her 'Victory' embodies the exhaustion of the winners in 1918. If her native Britain was beset by economic crisis and labour unrest after November 1918, as well as the growing ungovernability of Ireland, Russia, of course, was plunged into revolution by the strains of the Great War.

Elsewhere in Europe defeat in the war spelled the end of the traditional ruling monarchies, but in Russia the process went much further. After the abdication of the last Tsar, Nicholas II, in March 1917, the country rapidly descended into chaos. The Provisional Government tried to continue the war against the German invaders while promising democracy. Ordinary Russians saw no purpose to the struggle, which cost up to eight million lives. The German blockade also disrupted the supply of food and fuel to the big cities, especially the capital, Petrograd (St Petersburg). Hungry and disillusioned people there were ripe for agitation against the muddled would-be democrats led by Kerensky.

Many of the characters portrayed by Clare Sheridan were in foreign exile during the First World War and the uprising which overthrew the Tsar. A cynical marriage of convenience was agreed between the Zurich-based Lenin and the German High Command. Lenin was against the war and the Provisional Government in Russia which was still conducting it. The Germans wanted Russia out of the war at any cost so that they could concentrate their forces against the British and French in the West before the Americans intervened. Funded with German hard currency and transported across German-controlled territory in the famous sealed train (like a 'plague bacillus' according to cousin Winston), Lenin, Kamenev and others reached Petrograd in April 1917. With populist slogans demanding 'Peace, Land and Bread', Lenin succeeded in isolating the Provisional Government.

Whether his Bolshevik or 'majority' wing of the Marxist movement in Russia really represented the will of the people, or even of most Marxists there, must be doubted, but Lenin knew that politics is really a battle between active minorities. What mattered to him was that most people should see his party as the least obnoxious and remain passive while it fought for power with irreconcilable opponents. Lenin reversed Christ's teaching: to the

Communist leader, those who were not against him were for him. One of his first acts on seizing power on 7th November 1917 was to decree the distribution of land to the peasantry and soldiers in the still huge army on the front facing the Germans.

Most peasants in Russia accepted the division of land belonging to the better-off or the Church and feared a return to the old order. Soldiers deserted in millions, anxious not to be left out. At a stroke, Lenin undercut any chance of his political opponents being able to rely on the more than 80 per cent of the population who were peasants. Of course, as a good Marxist, Lenin had no intention of letting peasant private property survive any more than he tolerated capitalist ownership on a grand scale, but for the moment he needed to buy the peasantry's acquiescence, as he made clear to another early visitor, H. G. Wells (see note to page 89).

With the old imperial army gone, Lenin had dished any chance of a swift military coup to reverse his own seizure of power, but he also found Russia defenceless before the German army. Against the protests of Trotsky and Bukharin, Lenin forced through acceptance of the harsh terms of the Treaty of Brest-Litovsk in March 1918. He knew that his predecessor, Kerensky, had fallen because he carried on the war after the February Revolution in 1917. Confident that a worldwide crisis of capitalism was under way and that the rest of Europe would soon follow Russia into the Soviet fold, Lenin argued that the Bolshevik regime could afford to concede vast territories to Imperial Germany now because soon enough a revolution in Berlin would sweep away the Kaiser and install a pro-Soviet Communist government. When Wilhelm II fell in November 1918, and Germany sued for peace, revolution seemed unstoppable, but if the German army could not defeat the Western Allies it made mincemeat of its native Communists. Throughout Central Europe, the Red Flag flew but only briefly in the turbulent months after the end of the First World War.

So long as they were engaged in a life-and-death struggle with Germany, the Western Allies bitterly resented what they saw as Russia's desertion of the common cause. Many Westerners regarded Lenin as little better than a German agent. In later years Soviet propaganda greatly exaggerated Allied intervention on the side of the anti-Communist White armies in the Civil War, but at the time Lenin and Trotsky were all too well aware of Russia's weakness by comparison with the industrial West. It was the defeat of Germany which saved the Soviet regime: the British Prime Minister, David Lloyd George, no longer saw the men in Moscow as a serious threat to Western interests, unlike his cabinet colleague, Winston Churchill, who was the most vociferous advocate of intervention until Lenin was overthrown.

Like many subsequent Western leaders, Lloyd George could not conceive of politicians who really believed their own rhetoric. He thought that trade contacts and simply calming down the international atmosphere would persuade the Bolsheviks to abandon their declared aim of spreading worldwide revolution and throwing men like himself into what Trotsky had called 'the dustbin of history'.

Just as he was not averse to dealing with Ludendorff when desperate, Lenin saw nothing wrong with deceiving Western leaders into thinking that he shared their view that the Communist regime must turn 'normal' at some point. When the Red Army's invasion of Poland in August 1920 was routed outside Warsaw a few weeks before Clare Sheridan's arrival in Soviet Russia, Lenin recognised that his hopes that the Polish and other proletariats would rise up and fight alongside their Russian brothers were misplaced. The Catholic Polish peasants preferred rule by their own gentry to domination by foreign atheists.

In these circumstances, Lenin had sent two of his most trusted comrades from the Bolshevik underground movement of Tsarist Russia, Lev Kamenev and Leonid Krassin, to London, the capital of the most dangerous 'imperialist' power, to open trade negotiations with an eye to diplomatic recognition. As at Brest-Litovsk in 1918, Lenin wanted a breathing-space to build up Soviet power, but the apparent willingness of the Bolsheviks to talk about commercial matters helped to persuade the British Government that the long-awaited abandonment of the Communist folly was about to happen.

Clare Sheridan was sufficiently unusual for a lady of her class to take more than a passing interest in the strange, almost fabulous creatures that Kamenev and Krassin were to most upper-class Britons (and to lower-class ones too!). Far from being put off by their easy manners and un-English cosmopolitanism, she was attracted by their willingness to discuss the new world coming into being in Russia. How far she recognised that they saw her as a useful entrée into the world of high society and politics is unclear. Certainly, when she got to Moscow, Lenin made it apparent that he knew of her relationship with his arch-enemy, Churchill. Already in Russia itself before the Revolution the Bolsheviks had been happy to recruit scions of the aristocracy and wealthy into their ranks or to use them as agents of influence.

In fact, if the object of granting Clare Sheridan unprecedented access to the Bolshevik leaders was to use her in that way, they must have been disappointed. *Russian Portraits* is certainly not hostile, but it is by no means unadulterated adulation in what became the true fellow-travelling style. In any case, within a few years, Sheridan turned against the Communists and her writings in the later 1920s and 1930s carried all the more weight because of her uniquely early encounter.

Clare Sheridan's account of her easy relationship with first Kamenev and Krassin, then most of the other Bolshevik leaders, is convincing. Whatever their root-and-branch radicalism, they had all benefited from excellent educations and were widely travelled. Nor could they be called stuffy. The Bolshevik leaders were supremely confident of their role in history. Indeed, despite their temporary difficulties, they saw themselves as history's agents and on its winning side. But they were not immune to the pleasures of showing off in front of a pretty widow, especially one from the losing class.

Amid the galaxy of Bolshevik stars whom she met and portrayed, Sheridan missed the rising sun of Stalin. In 1920 he was still not general secretary of the Communist Party and so not yet in the real seat of power which he used after 1922 as the key position from which to control the whole Communist Party and therefore the Soviet state. In the autumn of 1920, Stalin was still under a cloud because his insubordination as political commissar of the Red Army's southern flank advancing into Poland had contributed to its historic defeat at the gates of Warsaw. It is a pity that he was missing from her collection of portraits, but his future victims are all the more interesting for appearing for once without his shadow.

The lesser characters too are full of interest. The American con-man, Vanderlip, remains mysterious apart from Sheridan's glimpses of him. Lenin perhaps let himself into the trick by presuming that Vanderlip was a Vanderbilt – an easy enough mishearing of which Vanderlip did nothing to disabuse the Soviet leader. Here at last was a gullible capitalist billionaire willing to invest in Soviet Russia to help its modernisation and also with the ear of President Harding. Lenin could not believe his luck! Vanderlip was happy to get out of Soviet Russia with a small advance on imports of technology which never came. No wonder Lenin turned to the committed socialist, Armand Hammer, when he next wanted to deal with a tame capitalist who might 'sell the rope with which he was going to be hanged'.

Unknown to Sheridan, even as she spoke to him, Lenin was beginning to doubt whether his attempt to introduce fully fledged Communism in one great leap after 1917 could work. By the end of 1920, even though organised resistance to the new regime had been crushed, the economy was in a downward spiral, famine haunted town and country alike. Within a few months, four million would be dead.

Sheridan's picture of Bolshevik Russia on the eve of Lenin's great retreat from War Communism and the adoption of the New Economic Policy in the spring of 1921 might seem naive at times, but its evident honesty helps us to understand the impact that the forging of a completely new social order made upon people from the West, not least the uneasily privileged. In any case, she

depicted the rationing of all foodstuffs and the valueless-
ness of money. Perhaps she misunderstood the thin
soups and light meals which she and Mikhail Borodin
ate to be typical rations, but at least she has none of
Bernard Shaw's perverse delight in being well fed during a Soviet famine ten years later. Her anecdote of the
unwillingness of the Cheka guards at the Kremlin to
accept a wad of worthless paper money as a tip was more
a reflection of their share in the *nomenklatura* system
which accorded special rations and rights to the Soviet
élite from the very beginning rather than any principled
Communist disdain for cash.

Although naive in describing an encounter with a
critic of the Soviet regime to her minder Borodin, at least
she made sure that he could not be identified. Sheridan
was not fully aware of the 'Red Terror' but she recognised
that the Bolsheviks could be ruthless. She also wit-
nessed their extraordinary secretiveness – Kamenev, for
instance, did not tell her that the painter Rosenfeld was
his brother – and security-consciousness. Her description of Trotsky's distant speech on Red Square is an early
example of the artificial and staged 'popular' meeting
which reached its apogee a dozen years later under
Stalin.

As an artist Sheridan naturally was interested in the
Soviet treatment of the arts. At the time, encouragement
of the *Proletkult* of radical modernists went hand in
glove with the promotion of the classics of the past, at
least in terms of opening theatres and galleries to the
poor (who were not always enthusiastic about this ex-
tension of privileges formerly reserved for the upper few
per cent). As things turned out, Sheridan's emphasis
on the respect of the new Soviet authorities for the

creations of the past, not least religious works of art, turned out to be optimistic. Many of the churches which she admired were demolished over the next decade or so, and their bells melted down and icons sold abroad (by Armand Hammer).

Based in Moscow and really staying within the narrow confines of the Kremlin district for most of her time, Sheridan enjoyed an unprecedentedly privileged access to the Soviet leaders but was also cut off from the reality of much of life beyond the city centre. None the less, Sheridan's *Russian Portraits* remains a fascinating picture of events at the centre of the embattled revolution, which for all the failure of its successors in our own time marked the decisive break in modern history after the French Revolution of 1789.

After her encounter with the Bolsheviks, Sheridan went on to travel widely and to portray many other famous men from Gandhi to Churchill, but her long life was a bitter symbiosis of creation and tragedy. In 1937 her son, Richard, died at the age of twenty-one. Just as she had come to sculpture after the death of a daughter, so she turned to tree-carving to commemorate her boy. She found comfort in conversion into the Catholic Church in 1945. She died in 1970 and is buried next to her memorial to her son at Brede Place, Sussex, but, as readers of this book will agree, she does not deserve to be forgotten.

FURTHER READING

Anita Leslie's *Cousin Clare* (London, 1976) is the only biography, but in addition to Clare Sheridan's own memoirs, especially *To the Four Winds* (London, 1957), her name crops up in many volumes of letters and diaries as well as in the autobiographies of her contemporaries.

The best biography of Lenin and portrait of the period remains Adam Ulam's *Lenin and the Bolsheviks* (London, 1966). The classic account of the Revolution and Civil War is W. H. Chamberlin's *The Russian Revolution* in two volumes (Princeton, 1987), but see also Richard Pipes' *The Russian Revolution* (London, 1991). For those interested in the culture of the time, the two volumes edited by William G. Rosenberg, *Bolshevik Visions: First Phase of Cultural Revolution in Soviet Russia* (2nd edition, Chicago, 1990), will be useful. The best guide to the city and culture of Moscow at the time is *Moscow, 1900–1930* edited by Serge Fauchereau (New York, 1988).

RUSSIAN PORTRAITS

BY CLARE SHERIDAN

MCMXXI

CLARE SHERIDAN IN THE RUSSIAN SHEEPSKIN HAT
GIVEN TO HER BY KAMENEFF IN MOSCOW

ILLUSTRATIONS

RUSSIAN PORTRAITS

FOREWORD

It is with deep apology that I venture to swell the ranks of those people who write their little books after their little visits to Russia.

In defence I can only say that this was not written for publication. I have always kept a diary, in monotonous as in eventful days. In publishing a record of my stay in Moscow I am submitting to pressure without which I would not venture on such a line. Mine is not the business of writing, nor are politics my concern: I went to Moscow where some portrait work was offered me.

There are people in England who are indignant at my doing Lenin and Trotsky. There were people in Moscow who were horrified because I had done Churchill, and expressed a desire to do d'Annunzio, but as a portraitist I have nothing to do with politics; it is humanity that interests me, humanity with its force and its weakness, its ambitions and fears, its honesty and lack of scruples, its perfection and its deformities.

There are of course people who are pleasanter to work for than others, people in whose environment one feels happier and more at ease.

RUSSIAN PORTRAITS

In this diary are written freely the impressions of a guest among people who have been much talked about.

From this point of view, and without any political pretensions, I offer it to whosoever it may interest.

RUSSIAN PORTRAITS

AUGUST 14TH, 1920. *London*.

According to Mr. Fisher's instructions I called on Mr. M— at his office at 10.30 and introduced myself.

He took me in a taxi to Bond Street to the office of Messrs. Kameneff and Krassin. We waited for about twenty minutes in an antechamber, and I had a certain melodramatic feeling. Here was I, at all events, in the outer den of these wild beasts who have been represented as ready to spring upon us and devour us! This movement that has caused consternation to the world, and these people so utterly removed from my environment, these myths of what seemed almost a great legend, I was now quite close to. Meanwhile the clerks in the office occupied my attention, they interested me as types, and I wondered about them, about exactly what in their lives had made them into Bolsheviks, and what sort of mentality it was, and whether the scheme which they upheld was a workable concern.

At the same time Mr. M— put me straight on a few points, and all the inaccuracies about Bolshevism that people like myself have gleaned, so that I was fairly prepared and protected against appearing too ignorant and foolish.

At last the word came and we were ushered into the office of Mr. Kameneff who received me amiably and smilingly. We started off almost immediately, in French, and discussed the subject of his being willing to sit to me. I then asked him if a Soviet Government had obliterated Art in Russia. He looked at me for a moment in astonishment, and then said: '*Mais non!* Artists are the most privileged class.'

I asked if they were able to earn a living wage. He replied that they were paid higher than the Government Ministers. He gave me fully to understand that Russia is most appreciative of Art and Talent, and is anxious to surround itself with culture.

He decided that the bust had better be started soon, as one never knew what might happen from one moment to the next, 'what caprice of Monsieur Lloyd George' might elect to send him out of the country at a moment's notice, so we decided on the following Tuesday at 10 a.m. Mr. Kameneff then took us downstairs to Krassin's office. Mr. Krassin seemed very busy and preoccupied, had someone in the room, and didn't quite know what I had come about, but he agreed to sit to me on the following Wednesday at 10 a.m.

AUGUST 17TH.

Kameneff arrived almost punctually at 10 a.m. for an hour, but he stayed till 1 o'clock, and we talked for the whole three hours almost without stopping. I do not know how I managed to work and talk so much. My mind was really more focussed on the discussion, and the work

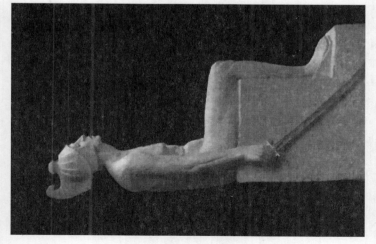

'VICTORY, 1918'

was done subconsciously. At all events when the three hours were ended, I had produced a likeness.

There is very little modelling in his face, it is a perfect oval, and his nose is straight with the line of his forehead, but turns up slightly at the end, which is a pity. It is difficult to make him look serious, as he smiles all the time Even when his mouth is severe his eyes laugh.

My 'Victory' was unveiled when he arrived and he noticed it at once. I told him it represented the Victory of the Allies, and he exclaimed: 'But no! It is the Victory of all the ages. What pain! What suffering! What exhaustion!' He then added that it was the best bit of Peace propaganda that he had seen.

We had wonderful conversations. He told me all kinds of details of the Soviet legislation, their ideals and aims. Their first care, he told me, is for the children, they are the future citizens and require every protection. If parents are too poor to bring up their children, the State will clothe, feed, harbour and educate them until fourteen years old, legitimate and illegitimate alike, and they do not need to be lost to their parents, who can see them whenever they wish. This system, he said, had doubled the percentage of marriages (civil of course), and it had also allayed a good deal of crime – for what crimes are not committed to destroy illegitimate children?

He described the enforced education of all classes – he told of the concerts they organise for their workmen, and of their appreciation of Bach and Wagner.

They have had to abandon (already!) the idea that all should be paid alike. Admitting that some are physically able to work longer and better than others, therefore there have to be grades of payment, and when great talent shows itself, *'cela merite d'être recompensé.'*

Chaliapin, who used to have the title of 'Artist to the Court', is now called 'The Artist of the People'. Chaliapin, I gathered, was a very popular figure.

After a while, Kameneff let drop a suggestion which did not fall on barren ground – he threw it out apparently casually, but in order, I believe, to see how I reacted to it. I had just been telling him that I had all my life had a love of Russian literature, Russian music, Russian dancing, Russian art, and he said, 'You should come to Russia.'

I said that I had always dreamed it – and that perhaps – who knows – someday . . .

He said, 'You can come with me, and I will get you sittings from Lenin and Trotsky.'

I thought he was joking, and hesitated a moment, then I said : 'Let me know when you are going to start, and I will be ready in half an hour.'

He offered to telegraph immediately to Moscow for permission.

AUGUST 18TH.

Krassin arrived at 10 a.m., and found me reading the papers, sitting on the seat outside the door. Like Kameneff, he stayed till 1 o'clock. He has a beautiful head, and he sat almost sphinx-like, severe and expressionless most of the time. We talked of course, but his French is less good than Kameneff's, and we broke into occasional German – it was a good mix-up, but we said what we wanted to say.

Kameneff had talked to him about me, and had told him of the project of my going to Moscow. I said nothing about it until he mentioned it.

What impresses me about these two men is their impassive imperturbability, their calm, and their patience. I suppose it is the race, or else that they learnt calm when they were prisoners in Siberia. It is such a contrast to almost every other sitter, who is restless, hurried and fidgety. Krassin is sphinx-like; he sits erect, his head up, and his pointed, bearded chin sticking defiantly out at an angle, and his mouth tightly shut. He has no smile like Kameneff, and his piercing eyes just looked at me impassively while I worked. It was rather uncanny.

Krassin is a Siberian. He explained to me that his father was a Government local official when he married his mother who was a peasant, and one of twenty-two children. He himself was the eldest of seven, and was brought up in Siberia.

At 1 o'clock I thanked him profusely for sitting so long and so well, and he seemed quite surprised at my stopping, and said : 'You have done with me?'

I explained that I had to catch a train, so, having swallowed a fish and some plums, I rushed down the alley to my taxi, pursued by Rigamonti who abandoned his marble chisel and carried my suitcase and hurled in some last things to me. I just caught the 1.50 at Waterloo, for Godalming, to stay two days with the Midletons.[1]

AUGUST 21ST.

I got back to the studio about midday to find a huge bunch of roses and the following note from Kameneff:

1   Earl Midleton, Peper Harow, Godalming, Surrey.

London, 21 Août

Chère Madame,

Je vous prie la permission de mettre ces roses rouges
aux pieds de votre belle statue de la Victoire.

Bien à vous,

L. K.

I did so, and when he came at about 4 o'clock to sit, I thanked him, but said that they were not red and that it was a pity. He looked as if he didn't quite understand, and said: 'Yes, they are red – red for the blood of Victory.' The sentiment was right, but he is colour blind, the roses were pink! I did not argue.

At about 5 o'clock S— L— walked in unexpectedly, and was very surprised and interested to find Kameneff, who was no less interested at hearing from S— L— that Archbishop Mannix is his guest, and I got a good innings at my work while these two talked together.

Kameneff and I dined later at the Café Royal, and then went on to a Revue, which was very bad, but the audience laughed a good deal, and Kameneff wondered at their childish appreciation of rubbish.

AUGUST 22ND.

Twelve hours with Kameneff!!!

He arrived at 11 a.m. with a huge album of photographs of the Revolution, very interesting. After looking at it he sat to me for an hour. We then lunched at Claridges'. After lunch we went for a taxi drive along the Embankment, and, passing the Tate Gallery, went in. It is being rearranged, but we found the Burne-Jones that Kameneff was looking for. He stood for a long time before 'The King and the Beggar-maid'. I suppose that in the new system all the beggar-maids are queens, and that the real kings sit at their feet.

At 4 o'clock we went to Trafalgar Square to see what was going on. The Council of Action were having a meeting. Kameneff assured me that he must not go near the platform, or be recognised by his friends, as he was under promise to the Government to take no part in demonstrations, nor to do any propaganda work. However, I dragged him by the hand to the outskirts of the crowd, and for no reason that I can explain, the shout went up, 'Gangway for speakers', and a channel opened up before us, and we were rushed along it. Happily for Kameneff, there was a hitch as we approached the platform. The crowd thought that a policeman was favouring us unduly, and getting us to the platform, and a youngish man said: 'Stop that, policeman, this is a democratic meeting' and tried to prevent us going any farther. For a while I felt the hostility of the people around me.

One of the speakers, referring to the spirit of 1914, said that we had given our husbands and sons then, but that we did not mean ever to give them again, and I, thinking of Dick, joined in the shouts of 'Never, never!' with some feeling, and I felt the atmosphere kindlier around me after that. When Lansbury tried to speak, he was acclaimed with cheers, and had to wait patiently while they sang 'For he's a jolly good fellow', and cheered him again.

He seemed to me to talk less of 'Class' and more of 'Cause'. Just for a second he paused when saying, 'What we have to do, is to stop—' I filled in the gap with 'Mesopotamia'. Whereupon the crowd shouted 'Here, here!' and 'God bless you!' After that I was one of them.

Then someone recognised Kameneff, and the whisper went round and spread like wildfire. The men on either side of him asked if they might announce that he was there, to which he answered a most emphatic 'No'.

When Lansbury had finished speaking, there was an appeal for money for the 'Cause'. It was interesting to watch the steady rain of coins, and very touching were the pennies of the poor. Lansbury buried his face in his hat for protection.

After that we went away, and a gangway was made for us, and all along the whisper went of 'Kameneff', and the faces that looked at us were radiant as though they beheld a saviour.

We took a taxi and drove to Hampton Court, and went into the park, to get away from the Sunday crowd. We sat on Kameneff's coat on the grass in the middle of an open space, and the air was heavy and the sun fitful, as though a storm impended. The distant elms were heavy green, and there was a great stillness and calm.

We talked about the meeting, and of the magnetism of a crowd. He noticed my suppressed excitement, for I had blood to the head! If we had been rushed to the platform, I could have spoken to the people, I am sure that I could. He said that he had been terribly moved to speak, and that it had been a great effort to hold back.

We talked and talked, and then some rain drops forced us to get up and return to the Mitre hotel for dinner. After dinner, the weather cleared, and we had a lovely hour and a half in a boat on the river. There was a three-quarter moon, and the water reflected the pink lights from the Chinese lanterns of the houseboats. From the garden of Hampton Court rose up what seemed to be a giant cypress tree, silhouetted against the dusk, and the reflection of it doubled its height. It was like something in Italy. I rowed the boat, which I loved doing, and Kameneff hummed Volga boatman songs. Or else we broke back into discussions, and then he forgot that he was steering, and we had several slight collisions, and narrow escapes from more serious ones!

It was a very successful evening, and we came back by the last train to Waterloo, still talking, chiefly about that impending and all-absorbing visit to Moscow, and we parted on my doorstep at a quarter to midnight.

AUGUST 24TH.

I felt ill, but got up early, expecting Krassin at 10 o'clock, but at 10 o'clock I got a telephone message to the effect that neither Krassin nor Kameneff could see me today, as the political crisis had caused a deluge of work.

Lloyd George at Lucerne had taken exception to the clause in the Russian Peace Terms demanding that the Polish Civic Militia should be drawn from the working classes. This they say is an infringement of the liberty of Poland. Truth to tell, it is the Polish success over the Red Army that has caused this diplomatic *volte-face*. However, that is too long to go into here.

At dinner time Kameneff telephoned to me that he at last had time to spare, and could he come and see me. I asked him to take pot-luck for dinner, and he arrived, a battered and worn fighting man, full of indignation, but still full of fight, and hope, and belief.

He stayed till 11, and said that he felt better. It was very still here, and the peace did him good. There may be a 'State of War' in a few days, and as things now stand,

16

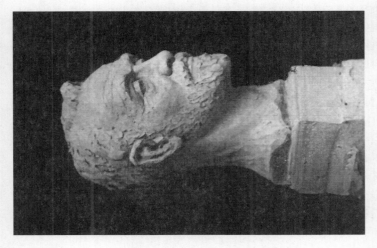

BUST OF KRASSIN

they all depart on Friday. Great excitement, as I shall go with them.

AUGUST 25TH.

Krassin gave me my second sitting at 5 p.m., and stayed till 7.30. I heard all the latest news. He's a delightful man, never have I done a head that I admired more. He seems to be strong morally, to a degree of adamant. He is calm, sincere, dignified, proud, without self-consciousness and without vanity, and scientific in his analysis of things and people. Eyes that are unflinching and bewilderingly direct, nostrils that dilate with sensitiveness, a mouth that looks hard until it smiles, and a chin full of determination.

AUGUST 26TH.

Krassin offered me a third sitting, and came again at 5.0 and stayed till after 7.0. War is averted, and he assures me that Kameneff under no excuse can possibly leave for Russia for a fortnight. I did not sleep much, waking up with the exclamation *'Partons! Partons!'* for if we do not get away for a fortnight, I shall have to keep my engagement on September 10th at Oxford with the Birkenheads to do F. E., and then I shall not get to Russia before my exhibition.

I worked hard, and Krassin's head is finished. I think it good. Sydney[1] came to see me after dinner, and we talked fantastically about Russia, and what it might or might not lead to.

He is terribly interested.

1   Sydney Russell Cooke.

AUGUST 27TH.

Kameneff came at 11.0 to give me a last sitting. He was in a much happier frame of mind, chuckling over Tchicherin's reply to Lloyd George, which is an impudent bit of propaganda work, and *all* the papers *have* to publish it because it is official.

I awakened this morning with an excited and tired feeling, my hands trembling, which I have never known before. Kameneff arrived in much the same condition. He talked politics and got excited and worked up and produced the quizzical frown that I wanted. I worked well, and absolutely changed the whole personality of his bust, which I think he liked.

He promised, incidentally, not to wait here two weeks, but says that he will start *not later* than next Friday. I wonder if he keeps his promises.

Peter[1] turned up with a girl, which disturbed the sitting and I felt more and more hectic, what with the difficulties and the battle of it, and knowing that it was the last sitting, and feeling dead beat, and having finally to stop for lunch.

We lunched with Sydney Cooke at Claridges'. I introduced them to each other, and we are going to stay with Sydney at his house in the Isle of Wight, for the weekend. Like all good foreigners, Kameneff expressed a desire, some days ago, to see the Isle of Wight. So we arranged to go – I could not therefore go to my beloved Dick,[2] but I sent him a crocodile by Peter, to compensate for my absence.

Dined with Aunt Jennie,[3] she has laryngitis, and

1 Oswald Frewen, my brother.
2 Richard Brinsley Sheridan, born September 20th, 1915.
3 Lady Randolph Churchill.

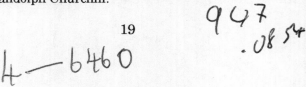

looked very ill. She asked me what new work I was engaged on, but I took good care not to mention either Russians or Russia.

In the course of conversation, she told me that I was being criticised as having too much freedom. I chuckled over this, as I visualised to myself the great band of people who grudge one that freedom, because they have not got it, and because they know that freedom counts above rubies.

I said to Aunt Jennie, 'And how is that grave condition of things, that dangerous "Liberty" going to be rectified? I am a widow, and earn my living, how is it to be otherwise ordered?'

She had no suggestion, it would have been obviously out of place to suggest re-marriage, which in fact is the only way of ending it, of ending everything, liberty, work, and my happiness, which is dependent on my work.

AUGUST 28TH.

I left the studio in a state of chaos, Smith being in the midst of casting the busts of Kameneff and Krassin. I felt a wonderful sensation of relief at these being finished, and the Victory also. Everything for the moment is finished, until I begin something new. And who will that be, I wonder?

Kameneff picked me up at 12.15 and we caught the 12.50 from Waterloo to Portsmouth. Sydney met us at the harbour and escorted us to his house on the Isle of Wight, near Newport. A very attractive journey across, as it was warm and calm weather. A motor met us at Ryde and took us to his house, seven miles. On arrival we flung ourselves down in the sun on the grass of the tennis-court. And after tea, as we lay full length on rugs,

BUST OF KAMENEFF

our heads leaning on the grassy bank behind us, and the sun gradually sinking lower and lower, Kameneff for over an hour told us the history of the Russian Revolution.

He told it to us haltingly, stumbling along in his bad French, wrestling with words and phrases, but always conveying his meaning and above all conjuring up the most graphic pictures, making us see with his eyes, live over the days with him, and know all the people concerned. He is amazingly forceful and eloquent.

We sat silent and spellbound. He began as far back as twenty years ago with the first efforts of himself and Lenin, Trotsky and Krassin. He described their secret organisations, their discoveries, their secrets, his months and years of prison, first in cells, then in Siberia – but long before he had finished, our dinner was announced, and we went in just as we were, to eat. The spell for the moment was broken, and though Kameneff did not again that evening resume the tale of the revolution, he did most of the evening's talking.

He described to us shortly, but vividly, the individuality and psychology of Lenin. There were others whose names I cannot recall. One I remember was Dzhirjinsky, the President of the Extraordinary Commission, a man turned to stone through years of *travaux forcés*, an ascetic and a fanatic, whom the Soviet selected as organiser and head of 'La Terreur'.

This is the man of whom Maxim Gorki wrote that one could see martyrdom crystallised in his eyes. He performs his arduous task, suffering over it, but with the conviction that he is helping toward an ultimate reign of peace and calm, towards which end every means is justified. The man sleeps in a narrow bed behind a curtain in his 'bureau', has few friends, and cares for no woman, but he is kind to children and considerate towards his fellow-workers when they are overworked or ill.

It is useless to try to tell any of Kameneff's stories, they require his individuality, and would lose in repeating. I only felt that it was a great waste that his audience should consist only of us two, when so many might have been enthralled.

AUGUST 29TH.

When I came down from breakfast I found the two men sitting over a fire. I accused them of 'frowsting', and carried them out to the garden, where Kameneff restarted his unconcluded tale of the Revolution, until we could bear the cold no more, so he finished it indoors in front of the fire. It is a marvellous narrative, pray God I may never forget it.

At 2.30, the afternoon having mended, we started off in an open car for the south of the island. On a hill overlooking the sea, with a lonely beach, we stopped, and made a long arduous descent. It was heavenly on the undulating beach of tiny rounded pebbles by the sea edge. Sydney and I paddled and Kameneff, who watched us, became thoroughly laughing and happy. When Sydney and I sat down on the beach and buried our feet in the pebbles, Kameneff began to write verses to me on the back of a five pound note.

I don't know what happened to the bank note, but Kameneff wrote four lines, and Sydney the other four, in French. Kameneff likened me to Venus, but Sydney was flippant, and said that the part of me that he liked best was my feet!

The scenery and the climb recalled Capri, but a faded Capri, without colour. Nevertheless, one recalled the feeling of joy that one had at Capri, and Kameneff was much impressed by the beauty and the peace of it, and said how distant politics seemed, and how non-existent Mr. Lloyd George!

After a while we regretfully went on, stopping only for a tea-picnic on a common by a lonely road.

SEPTEMBER 2ND. *Brede Place.*

I have been here since Monday. Papa is away in Ireland fishing, Mamma is here and believes that I am still going yachting and that a telegram will call me away at any minute. As no wire has yet come and I cannot bear the suspense, I have decided to go up to London for the day, and shall go straight to Kameneff's office from the station so that I shall know soon whether we start for Russia on Saturday or not. If we do I shall not come back here.

I wonder what it will be. Tonight, when I said good night to him, Dick clung to me more even than usual, and we talked together for a long time. He held me tight. I was kneeling on the ground beside his bed with my arms round him. He said that he could not bear to let me go tomorrow, and that he would tie me up to a wall. He was so very sweet, and I felt a great reluctance at leaving him.

SEPTEMBER 3RD.

I went up to London and drove straight to the Bolshevik office in Bond Street, and left my luggage waiting outside in the taxi. Unlike the previous occasion, I was not shown straight in to Kameneff. I sat down and

24

waited in the outer room which was full of men, six or seven of them, and they began discussing me in Italian, French, German and Russian! I tried to look dignified and aloof, and was, I am sure, a great failure as a Bolshevik. All my English conventional breeding took hold of me. Then later Peter came to fetch me, thinking that I had finished my interview, and then, having him to talk to, I felt better. Later an eighth man appeared with a number of papers and the garrulous crowd became of a sudden serious, placed themselves round a table, and seemed to hold a sort of council.

At this moment Klyschko passed by the open door, and espying me called Peter and me into his room to wait. I asked him why there were so many people in the other room, but he only shrugged his shoulders.

At last I was told that both Kameneff and Krassin wanted to see me, and I was shown into Krassin's office. I learnt in a moment what I had feared, that our journey is not for tomorrow. Moscow has answered his application too late. There was just a faint chance left, for a telegram from Moscow was being deciphered at that moment, but it was almost too slight to count upon.

Krassin asked if he might bring his wife and daughters to the studio at 4 o'clock, and then Kameneff took me up to his office. He held out real hopes of starting next week.

As soon as Krassin and his very attractive family, but slightly alarming wife, had left, I went to see X— whom I thought was in a position to get the visa I want for Reval. My passport is all in order to Stockholm, but Klyschko has failed to get the Esthonian visa, because it is necessary to get the Foreign Office approval to do so.

After three-quarters of an hour's talk with X— I realised that it was hopeless; he merely shared the general prejudice. It confirms me in my decision not to take anyone else into my confidence, except Sydney and S— L—. They are the only two who have got the spirit to understand.

But how I want that Esthonian visa – it is worth an effort to get it, instead of starting with an uncertainty.

X— explained to me at great length, and kindly, why he did not want me to go. He said that he believed a complete change of Government policy was impending, which would make my position in Russia untenable, and moreover that I should be in great danger of being shot as a spy. He told me what he thought of Lenin and Trotsky (it seemed very much what other people think), he said that Kameneff was no better than the rest, and that a Russian was capable of turning even upon a friend. Finally he asked me *why* I wanted to go. I claimed an artist's zeal in wishing to do a bust of Lenin and to bring his head back in my arms!

He then wanted to know why 'they' wanted to take me, to which I could give no clear answer, having wondered somewhat myself. He then tried to draw me on the subject of Bolshevism, and asked me: 'What do you gather is the final and ultimate object of the Bolsheviks?'

It was a difficult question – I thought for a moment, and then I said: 'They are very great idealists; it may be an unpractical and unworkable idealism, but that does not alter it.'

He was surprised at this, and said in a low voice, almost more to himself than to me: 'Are they as clever as that?' – by which I suppose he meant, had they really been clever enough to take me in!

At the end of it all I said to him: 'You have seen in the papers that H. G. Wells is going to Russia?'

He said that Wells could look after himself. I claimed to be equally fit to do so, to which he replied: 'So you still want to go?'

I explained that I was prepared for anything. He seemed surprised, but practically assented to try and get my passport put in order for me, and asked me to go and see him again next week.

I got back in time to dine with Kameneff at 'Canuto's'. After dinner, it being a lovely warm evening, we took an open taxi, and I suggested driving to Hampstead Heath. Arrived there, we left the taxi on the main road, whilst we went on foot off a side road on to a rough sandy track, quite away from people and lights.

On a bank I spread my white fur coat, and we sat there for an hour or more. It was very beautiful. The tall pine stems stood out against the glowing sky of distant, flaring London. The place was full of depth and distance, and night mystery. I talked to Kameneff about my conversation with a friend, who was a serious, intelligent man, and told him of his opinion that I should be in danger of my life. I added that I was prepared to take the risk, but that I should regret my children being orphans. Kameneff answered me half amused, half irritated.

He said it was such nonsense that he felt a great desire to start immediately, so as to show me the truth, and so that I might come back and prove to all and sundry how ignorant they are of real conditions.

He considered that no matter *what* line the Government adopted here (and he was prepared for Lloyd George to do anything at any moment), it would not affect me. I should be regarded purely as an artist, international and non-political.

Then laughing, he said that he would have me put against a wall, arms crossed on breast (not blindfolded, that was a convention of the aristocrats), with a firing party before me, and then he would save me at the last moment. Then I should have lived through every thrill, and my friends would not be disappointed.

He told me, incidentally, that Wrangel is defeated and discredited. (X—, having just told me that Wrangel had won the peasants over to him, and that he had a scheme of moderate Government, and was likely to rouse a counter-Revolution and depose the present lot.)

So I said to Kameneff: 'Where is truth?'

And he answered: 'There is no truth in the world, the only truth is in one's own heart.'

SEPTEMBER 9TH.

My birthday, and the most hectic day of my life!

In the morning I worked more or less calmly. The 'Victory' was just being finished, Smith was chipping away the last remains of mould. Rigamonti, under my direction, was punching the block of Princess Pat., so that marble chips flew like shrapnel in all directions. Meanwhile, Hart came to get my last orders about marble pedestals for unfinished bronzes, and on top of all Fiorini turned up.

He was terribly hurt because I have given the heads of Kameneff and Krassin to Parlanti to cast. He had dreamed of doing them – he had a Bolshevik workman in his foundry, who asked every day when those heads were coming. He would have cast them, he said, for nothing, just for the honour and glory of doing them. I felt terribly badly about it. The little Italian man is such an enthusiast, and he met Kameneff here, who shook hands with him, and Fiorini felt about it as most other people would about their King.

Moreover, on that occasion, he hid behind a pedestal, and remained so quiet for a quarter of an hour, watching me and my sitter, that I forgot that he was there. But because I understood from him that he had as much work as he could get through for me in time for my exhibition, I had given the heads to Parlanti, who promised them in time.

I hope that I comforted him by promising to give him duplicates to cast, as presents for Kameneff and Krassin, the which I had had no intention of doing, and can ill afford, but to cheer up Fiorini, I will do it.

Then the telephone went and Klyschko announced to me that it was all decided – Kameneff is starting on Saturday morning, has reserved places, and I have nothing to do but get my ticket. I said that I was having difficulties over my passport, and he explained to me that all I need is the visa via Kristiania to Stockholm, and that at Stockholm the Esthonian Legation would see me through.

I dined with Sophie Wavertree and F. M. B. Fisher. He walked home with me; he it was who originally brought me into this wonderful new world.

SEPTEMBER 10TH.

Kameneff telephoned at breakfast. He is really starting tomorrow.

At 10.15, a wire from Sydney to say that he is arriving from Scotland, at 5 o'clock.

11.30, to Barclays Bank, cashed £100.

11.40, to Cooks', bought my ticket.

12 o'clock, to Bond Street Office, saw Kameneff. He says it doesn't matter about a passport, that he can push me through from Stockholm.

1 o'clock, bought a hat in South Moulton Street.

2 o'clock, back at studio. Wrote letters all afternoon.

4.30, hair washed and cut.

7 o'clock, back to studio, packed and dined.

10.30, Sydney came, and while we were talking Kameneff rang up to say he had a few short hours ago had his interview with Lloyd George, and that he gathered from the interview that he, Kameneff, leaves tomorrow, not to return – this was to warn me – but he told me to come all the same.

I rang up S— L—, who could hardly believe that I am really starting. He came round to see me, and we talked far into the night.

SEPTEMBER 11TH.

Mr. Krassin, and most of the 128 New Bond Street staff, were at St. Pancras to see us start. Krassin presented me with a big box of chocolates tied up with red ribbons. We were rather a conspicuous group on the platform, and I feared every second to meet someone whom I knew travelling, possibly to York, on the same train.

S— L— was there to wish me God-speed, and Sydney, who is staying with friends near Newcastle, and came down yesterday to spend my last evening with me, travelled back to Newcastle with us. Rigamonti turned up unexpectedly, which touched me very much.

Sydney, fulfilling his reputation as an organiser, discovered that there were two trains going to Newcastle, and that the next one which left a little later had a restaurant car, so we transferred our luggage from the one to the other, and in the process I lost my handbag, which had a hundred pounds in it in bank notes, all I possess in the world. It caused me some agitation, but Kameneff was quite calm and seemed to think that money was not very important, and that I should not have much need of it in Russia.

To my intense relief, however, Sydney found the case at Newcastle, in the lost property office, it travelled ahead of us on the other train.

Sydney came to the ship with us, I don't think he believed in the reality of my journey until he saw me safely past the passport officials.

I certainly felt no sense of security until the steamer left the quay-side. There was something indescribably exciting and clandestine about slipping away without anyone knowing.

For some time Kameneff and I stood on deck to see the last of England, with her Turner sky. The sunset was golden haze, and Kameneff said: 'It looks mysterious, that land, doesn't it?' But to me it was just the old world wrapped in a shroud. Mystery lay ahead of us in the new world that is our destination.

Now for the first time I had leisure and calm in which to think over what I am doing. There persist in my mind faint echoes of warnings, but I must have no misgivings, it seems to me unlikely that Kameneff would invite me to go to his country if I were likely to be either unhappy or in danger there. He must know what he is doing and what he is taking me to. There are moments in life when it is necessary to have blind faith.

SEPTEMBER 12TH. *S.S. 'Jupiter', Bergen, Norway.*

It is 9.45 p.m. We have just this moment come along the quay-side at Bergen. We are not to land until tomorrow morning. The crossing has been wonderful; as calm as a lake the whole way.

I have a cabin for three all to myself, there are very few people on board. It is as comfortable as a yacht. The only fellow traveller with whom we have spoken is an American, calling himself Comrade Costello. He reports for the Federated Press. A very keen journalist, typically American, and one who does not allow the grass to grow under his feet.

For an hour this afternoon I acted as interpreter between him and Kameneff. I had to ask about strange people and strange things, that I knew nothing about. I had not even heard of Debs before.

I expect that I shall have a pretty good knowledge of all the Revolutionary Leaders in all countries before long.

Kameneff had a cigarette in my cabin this evening, and we discussed Philosophy, Religion, and Revolution. It surprised me very much that he does not believe in God. He says that the idea of God is a domination and that he resents it, as he resents all other dominations. He talked nevertheless with great admiration of the teachings of Christ, Who demanded poverty and equality among men, and Who said that the rich man had no more chance of the Kingdom of Heaven than a camel of passing through a needle's eye.

SEPTEMBER 13TH. *Grand Hotel, Kristiania, Norway.*

Today might have been many days, and we might have been crossing the world.

The train left Bergen at 8.15 a.m. We had a compartment to ourselves with big windows.

Slowly from Voss the train climbed higher and higher. The higher we went the less vegetation there was. Big trees became smaller trees, and then dwarf trees, and then shrubs, until finally there was only the little low creeping juniper. There were rocks and boulders, falling torrents and cold, still lakes, and in the shadow of the mountain great patches of eternal snow that never melt.

This morning in the breakfast car we eagerly asked for news, being unable to read Norwegian. The man who was reading the paper informed us, in broken English, that the coal situation was exactly the same, and the Lord Mayor of Cork not dead yet, and with that summary we had to rest content.

Later in the morning, the dining-car attendant sought us out, and armed with a newspaper said: 'Have you heard the news?' He then made a bow and asked: 'Mr. Kameneff – yes?' and showed him a photograph of K. in the morning's paper, and the information that he had left England, and was on his way to Russia. That settled it, Kameneff was recognised, and the car attendant spread the information. After that, whenever we walked the platform of a station, we were the cynosure of all eyes.

At luncheon Kameneff asked the car attendant, who spoke Russian so well, where he had learnt it. The answer was that fifteen years ago he had spent two years as a waiter in Petrograd. Kameneff told him that Russia had changed considerably since then, and that he ought to go and see it. The attendant with a deferential smile said that he would be afraid to.

At Finse, the highest point, where we were on a level

with the mountain summits, and where snow lay round us and below us, the train stopped for ten minutes. We got out and walked about, and I took my kodak. Beyond the platform on the sloping bank a granite monolith stood up grimly against the snow-patched distance and, to my surprise, engraved upon it were the names of Captain Scott and all his party, with the date, and the announcement that they had started from Norway for the South Pole. It was rather *émotionant* finding it so unexpectedly, and so remote.

At 10 p.m., we steamed into Kristiania, where we were met by Litvinoff. I had visualised a small, sharp-faced, alert man. Instead I found a big, square, amiable, smiling man. He informed us that there was not a room to be had at the Grand Hotel, and turning to me, added in English: 'If you want rooms in the Grand Hotel you will have to secure them through the British Legation.' We all laughed, and I said : 'We are not making much use of the British Legation on this trip.'

As we entered the Grand Hotel and stepped into the lift, I caught the sound of string-band music, which characterises the Grand Hotels and Ritz-Carltons of Europe, and suggests all that side of life with which we on this trip are not quite in harmony. Litvinoff accommodated me in the room of one of his secretaries. I felt rather strange, lonely, and lost, especially when questioned by one of them as to my work and plans.

Had I been working in the Soviet office in London? I felt rather at a disadvantage, having to explain that I was merely an artist who had done portraits of Kameneff and Krassin (who, by the way, they spoke of as Comrade), and that I hoped to get through to Russia with Kameneff to do some portraits there.

I felt, as they looked at me, that I did not look much like a sculptor. They proceeded to tell me that no British passports were being issued, and that any amount of people were being held up here. Very cheerful! By this time I had drunk three cups of excellent tea out of a tumbler, and it was nearly midnight, so I suggested bed, apologising at the same time for making use of their room and necessitating their discomfort.

It being now 1 o'clock, I propose to sleep, though I am only wrapped in my rug, for the bed is not made up for me, and I do not like sleeping in other people's sheets! The noise in the street is perfectly infernal and Kameneff and Litvinoff are still talking in the next room on my other side.

SEPTEMBER 14TH. *Kristiania*.

Slept very well, wrapped in my rug. Woke up at 9 o'clock, and had breakfast in bed. Had looked forward to a bath, but the sour-faced hotel maid says there are too many gentlemen who want it, and so I cannot have one. This does not seem an adequate reason for denying it to me, and I rather suspect it is part of a general boycott of Bolsheviks.

While I was breakfasting, Kameneff looked in with the morning papers, which have come out with headlines and photographs of him. One describes him as having arrived 'with a lady, tall and elegant, who carried in one hand a "Kodakaparat" and in the other a box of sweets – she does not look Russian, and was heard to speak in French.'

At luncheon I met Mrs. Litvinoff, and was surprised to find that she is English, a friend of the Meynells and of H. G. Wells. She has short black hair, and is unconventional. She did not seem to be very political or revolutionary. The third baby is imminent.

After luncheon, we made an expedition outside Kristiania to the wireless station, which is on the top of a wooded hill from which there is a magnificent view. Misha, the eldest child, a boy of four, accompanied us. He is unruly, wild-eyed, and most attractive, the embodiment of Donatello's laughing boy. He says: 'What for is my father a Bolshevik?' and tells his mother to ring the bell for the maid, and not to do any work herself.

Litvinoff adores him and throws him about and makes him stand on his head. Coming home Litvinoff and I, hatless, ran races down the hill. To my great humiliation he outran me. He is a heavy man and I run well, but he was not even out of breath.

On the way back in the open car, they all sang Russian folk songs in a chorus. Bolsheviks are a very cheerful species.

We reached the hotel just in time to pick up our luggage and catch the train for Stockholm.

There were real cordial good-byes all round. Litvinoff said that if I did not get through from Stockholm, I must come back to Kristiania and he would send someone with me to take me through Murmansk, but Mrs. Litvinoff said that I should get through from Stockholm. 'That sort of person always gets what she wants' she said, but gave no further comment, and I am wondering what sort of person I am.

The two secretaries gave me messages for friends in Moscow, and seemed very envious of anyone going back. One of them (with most beautiful chestnut hair) held forth to me on the great difference the Revolution had brought in the position of women. She is an ardent

Communist, and works 10 hours a day with a willing heart and little pay. She added as a last appeal: 'Go and see for yourself, and then say nice things about us when you get back to England.'

SEPTEMBER 15TH. *Stockholm, Sweden.*

We arrived at 8.30 a.m., and were met at the station by Frederick Ström, head of the left-wing Socialist party of Sweden. It was an interesting contrast to my arrival in former years when the Crown Prince himself used to meet me and take me in a royal car to the Palace. I felt a great sadness as I passed that old Palace, and the windows of Princess Margaret's rooms which I knew so well. The days when I used to stay there seemed very long ago and of another world.

We drove to the Grand Hotel which, however, proved to be full, but we were not at a loss: we drove off to a perfectly charming apartment belonging to the Krassins, but which in their absence is inhabited by a Comrade Juon.

There we were most courteously received, and given a splendid breakfast.

Juon is about six feet and a half high, and broad in proportion, with a black beard and a kindly expression. His eyes have exceptionally big pupils, which give a curious gleam and keenness to his expression. His brother in Russia is a well-known painter.

Conversation between the two was mostly in Russian. I am beginning to cultivate a detached feeling, and I do not expect to understand much during the next few weeks, except through my eyes.

While we were breakfasting the Grand Hotel telephoned to place a suite of rooms at our disposal, so we returned there, and the hotel authorities were most civil.

From that moment there ensued a hectic period. Series of newspaper reporters arrived, and had to be given interviews. Comrades came, and stayed – there seemed to be people revolving perpetually. Some of them only understood German, others struggled in bad English, yet others in French; the whole conversation was mixed up with Swedish and Russian, so that one's head reeled.

Among all these people, one figure stands out more clearly than the rest. This is Rjasanoff, a man about seventy, with a Greek profile, a beard that sticks out defiantly and hawk's eyes. He has a dominating personality. He has done five years of solitary confinement in a cell for the cause. He was charming to me, and his expression lost some of its battle and became even kindly when he looked at me.

Another man who stands out in my mind is a Communist poet called Torré Norman, who has translated Rupert Brooke.

Mr. Ström accompanied me to the Esthonian Consulate to get my Reval visa. There were, as I expected, endless difficulties, and nothing was settled, and tomorrow the boat leaves at 4 o'clock so that there is not much time. I feel pretty confident that all will end well. It is not possible that there can be any other ending.

We were a big party lunching in the restaurant and attracted a good deal of attention. After lunch we all went to Skansen and had tea there.

In the evening, Kameneff had to go out and keep an appointment, and while he was away I wrestled on the telephone with reporters, trying to ward off interviews until the morrow. At 10 p.m., Kameneff came back and we dined in the sitting-room; he was pretty dead beat. Even then a reporter came to the door and asked for an interview, but I insisted that he *must* be put off until the next day, and Kameneff, rather willingly I think, gave in.

SEPTEMBER 16TH.

This morning I telephoned to the Palace and asked for the Crown Prince. Kameneff asked me if I were right to risk it. He said that I might be very ill received in view of the company I was in, but I explained that he was one of the most democratic Princes in Europe.

Prince Gustav's surprise was indeed pretty great. He was enormously interested and amused, and asked me to lunch, and to come at midday: so as to get a good talk first.

Kameneff listened to our conversation with some amusement. He told me afterwards that he liked 'the tone'. I wonder whether he had expected me to be different.

I asked the Prince as a favour that Princess Margaret's maid, Amy, might come out shopping with me. She came and fetched me, and was a tremendous help, as she knew where to take me, and did all the talking in Swedish.

I left her to collect my parcels, as it was nearly midday, got a taxi, and told him to drive to 'The Palace'. He looked vague, and did not understand. I said: 'Palace! Kronprinzen.' He nodded assent and drove off in a direction that I knew was not towards the Palace. We fetched up in a street in front of the Kronprinzen Hotel. It was hopeless to argue – I plunged into the hotel and asked for someone who spoke English and explained my dilemma, to the intense amusement of the hotel officials, and of the taxi driver when it was explained to him.

The Prince looked very lonely in those big rooms, and they were extraordinarily vibrant and reminiscent of *her*. He made me sit down and tell him all about my plans and my adventure, and fell thoroughly into the spirit of the thing. He said that I was quite right, if my exhibition at Agnew's for October was all organised, not to sacrifice the chance of this experience on that account. He thought the expedition a dangerous one, but sensibly admitted that that was my concern and no one else's.

He asked me, of course, a number of questions as to what sort of men Kameneff and Litvinoff were. I could not help being perfectly frank, and telling him my sincere impressions.

While I was there Kameneff telephoned to say that the Consulate of Esthonia had given me my visa.

At luncheon, the lady-in-waiting and the A.D.C.'s seemed rather bewildered. It certainly must have appeared fantastic to them, accustomed to the dull routine of Court life, to be entertaining someone who was on the way to Russia with Kameneff to model the heads of Lenin and Trotsky.

The Prince was overwhelming in his desire to help my material comforts. He telephoned for biscuits, and two large tins arrived, also cigarettes. He wrote out his prospective trip, with dates, to Athens and Italy, in hopes that possibly we may meet if I come back that way.

Finally he escorted me to the taxi that awaited me in the court-yard, and wished me luck and God-speed.

I returned to the Grand Hotel, and found an alarming crowd of Comrades lunching with Kameneff in his sitting-room, but we had to leave almost immediately to catch our boat for Reval.

SEPTEMBER 17TH. *Hango, Finland*.

It is evening, we have just put in at Hango, a Finnish port. No one is allowed off the ship, by order of the Port authorities. Finland is not yet at peace with Russia, and Kameneff would probably be arrested if he set foot on shore. The last time that he walked into Finnish territory in 1917, not knowing that the Whites were in possession of the town, he was put in prison for three months, and by a miracle was not shot. So far we have had a pretty good journey; the little boat has hugged the coast of the Aland islands. We have had to put into Hango for the night, because we can only steam by day on account of the floating mines between here and Reval that have not yet been cleared.

I have spent half the day in my cabin sleeping, the other half on deck talking. I have lost all track of days and dates; we seem to have been journeying for ever.

There are no pleasure trippers or any of the idle curious on board. Everyone practically is bound for Russia, and we look at one another curiously, wondering what each other's mission is. There are Comrades returning, and there are journalists, traders and bankers; people who hope to get through from Reval, people who probably *will*, and others who certainly will not.

Kameneff is watched by everyone, and we have made innumerable acquaintances. Already there is around us a little group of friends, whom one has the feeling of having known a long time. Tomorrow we go on to Reval. It seems to me too wonderful and unbelievable that I am really on this boat of fears and dreams: fears of not getting on board, and dreams of the world into which it would sail with me.

SEPTEMBER 18TH. *Reval, Esthonia.*

At dawn we left Hango, but there was such a wind blowing that the ship anchored just at the entrance of the harbour, and for a few hours we swung round. No one complained of delay and no one seemed to be in a hurry. There was no attempt to keep a scheduled time: a calm atmosphere of fatalism, which is probably Russian, seemed to hang over us.

The sun was shining brilliantly when we finally set out to sea, and I was having a most interesting conversation with Mr. Aschberg, a Swedish banker, who did me the compliment of talking to me on political economy, of which I understood nothing. He told me interesting things about Bolshevik business transactions with Germany, in which it seemed that the Bolsheviks were alienating the German workers by negotiating with the German capitalists.

In my own mind I did not see how they could do otherwise, but my ignorance on these things is so great, that I try to learn all I can without giving myself away by asking too many questions. It is a slow process, but I have hopes. The mere fact of being under the wing of a man like Kameneff, and bound for Russia, seems to make people talk to me as if I were a man. It is a great comfort no longer to meet people on a social or superficial ground. There were people even who talked to me on most obscure subjects, and asked for my intercession for them with Kameneff!

At sunset we steamed into Reval, where the pointed towers and the sound of old bells as in Italy awakened one to a new atmosphere that was no longer Scandinavian. A motor met us at the quay, the only motor there, and a man who had crossed with us, and whom I suspected of being a British agent, said to me ironically as he drove away in a droshki: 'How very smart and distinguished of you to have a motor—'

Kameneff's boy of twelve met us, and there were two small children as well, belonging to Gukovski, the Soviet representative at Reval. They took up most of the room that was needed for luggage. Alexandre Kameneff had to stand on the step outside, and a soldier of the Red Army on the other. Thus our curious car-load made its way, hooting loudly through mediaeval tortuous streets.

What followed is rather nebulous in my mind. I was very tired and the town very dark; there were stars overhead, but no street lamps. We drove to some bleak building called the Hotel Petersbourg, which seemed to be the Bolshevik G.H.Q. It was dirty and grim, and full of strange-looking people who talked no language that I understood. They looked at me strangely; a great many hands shook mine. Kameneff was too busy to explain to me what our plans were, or what was going to happen next, or maybe he forgot that I could not understand. He was too surrounded for me to be able to ask him any questions, so I just looked vague, waited about and followed, relying on my eyes to convey the explanations that my ears were denied. Kameneff was the centre of perpetual discussions in which everyone spoke at the same moment, very quickly and very loud. At first I suspected a most agitating State Council, but it turned out to be merely a discussion as to where we should have supper. Finally it was decided that we should go to the apartment in an hotel where the wife of a Comrade would look after us. Off we went on foot over cobble-stones. The streets were full of people who moved like shadows, and one could only see faces when they passed the glare of a lighted doorway. We followed along in couples. At my side was Alexandre Kameneff, a nice boy and friendly, but he could only talk Russian.

We got to the hotel (such an hotel, more like a wayside inn). We were taken to the Comrade's apartment, where his wife received us with great cordiality and talked to me in good French.

There was a samovar, and we had excellent tea with lemon in it, and some cold smoked salmon on thick slices of buttered bread. Kameneff and the two Comrades were too absorbed in their discussion to eat anything. One Comrade was telling something, Kameneff took notes, and our host, a small nervous man, rolled bread pellets.

Madame, in an even voice, plied me with questions:

'When did you leave London?'

'How long did you take from Stockholm to Reval? Oh, dear, a day and a half late! We have no news here, tell me some.'

'Is Comrade Kameneff really *chassé* from England?'

'Is it true that Krassin will soon follow?'

'What pretty hair you have, mademoiselle. Is it naturally that colour? Does it curl naturally so?'

'Is there a famine in England? I hear there is no longer sugar or butter? But there will be a famine when your strike begins?'

'What, you have not a macintosh with you?'

'Nor an umbrella?'

'Nor thicker shoes than that?'

'But do you not know there is nothing to be had in Russia?'

44

'You have goloshes? That is good.'

'And soap? Yes, they will do your washing if you give them soap to do it with—'

Kameneff left us to attend a meeting elsewhere. It was now pretty late, and I was tired; the room was small, and full of smoke and food. When I had finished my tea, Alexandre Kameneff and the soldier who had not left us since our arrival took me back to the headquarters. I did not know what was to become of me, and no one understood me. The dimly lit corridors were crowded with strange loungers. I was shown into a grim room where portraits of Lenin and Trotsky adorned the walls, and there I sat silently among people I could not talk with. After a while, to my intense relief, Kameneff appeared. In this strange *milieu* in which I was so utterly lost, Kameneff seemed to me the oldest and the only friend I had in the world, and I metaphorically clung to him as a drowning man to a straw. Somebody in the crowd, taking pity on my helplessness, or else wondering what I was asking for in three unknown languages, had sent him to me. He asked what on earth I was doing there. As if I knew! I followed him to another room, bigger and fuller of people, who all looked very serious and sat in a circle. The meeting went on, and I sat obscurely in a corner wondering whether, if I understood Russian, I should be allowed to be there. At last, bored by watching them and learning nothing from it, I got out a pencil and paper from the hand-case I had with me and wrote a letter to Dick. It was the last place from which I could post a letter and the last time I could write letters uncensored. I wrote to Dick from my heart, thinking of him at that moment in bed, so very far away, looking so round and pink, and with one arm outside the bedclothes. In spirit I was kneeling by his bedside and kissing the little bare arm. Dick and Margaret both know that when I am away from them I come in spirit in the night, and they often find a rose petal or a bud, or maybe a tiny feather, something very light, that I leave on the pillow to prove that I have been. Never had I been more with them in spirit than this night, when I felt so lonely and bewildered. Later on I wrote an apology to F. E., explaining why I had not turned up at Charlton to do his bust. It was one of the things that I felt rather badly about, for I had left England the very day that I was due at the Birkenheads'. I could not at that time explain, and they must have thought me so very rude. It is funny that none of these people, not even Kameneff, have heard of F. E., either as Smith, Lord Birkenhead, or Lord Chancellor. Chancellor of the Exchequer they understand, but no other Chancellor.

When at last the meeting was over, I was introduced to Gukovski, and gathered that we were in his room. He is a little bent man, who broke his back some time past in a motor accident. He has red hair and beard, and small narrow eyes that look at one with close scrutiny, and give one a shivery feeling. He asked me what my mission was, and when I had told him he said: 'Do you think that you are going to get Lenin to sit to you?' I did think so, and his eyes twinkled with merriment. 'Well you won't!' he said and chuckled.

Kameneff went off to converse on the telephone with Tchicherin at Moscow, and did not come back. I waited and waited, and Gukovski began packing a trunk; he was evidently coming with us. I watched him, a man's packing is always a rather interesting and pathetic sight, but even that ceased to interest me after a while, and I became conscious of a feeling bordering on tears and sleep. Where on earth was Kameneff, and why didn't he come back, or else explain to me how long this waiting was to go on. After a while I discovered that Gukovski's secretary, a young man called Gai, could speak perfectly good English. From him I learnt that our train was leaving 'about midnight' for Moscow, and that I could go to it any time I liked and find my sleeper. I ought to have known this long before as it was already nearly midnight. I made Alexandre Kameneff and the soldier take me to the station immediately. Of course when I got there the train was nowhere to be found – it was in a siding – and I sat down on a stone step and waited, thankful at least for the fresh air and the absence of glaring lights. When our 'wagon-de-luxe' finally appeared it was the best that I have ever seen. It had been the Special of the Minister for Railways, and was very spacious and comfortable. As soon as Kameneff, Gukovski and his little girl joined us, the train started and we had a midnight supper of tea and caviare.

SEPTEMBER 19TH.

All night we have journeyed, and all day. It is now evening. Our special train has stopped at a wayside station for three hours to await the Petrograd train, on to which we shall link for Moscow. Then we shall travel again all night and arrive at our destination tomorrow morning.

It has been a beautiful day of sunshine. I crossed the frontier riding on the engine. The front of our car has a verandah from which one can get a beautiful view. We crossed two wide rivers on temporary bridges, as the original ones lay in debris below us, having been blown up by Yudenitch in his retreat last year after his attack on Petrograd. The woods on either side of the river were full of trenches, dug-outs and barbed wire. I had tea and bread and caviare at 9 a.m. and the same thing at 3 p.m. and again at 7. There is no restaurant car; we have brought our own food with us in a hamper. There are other things to eat besides caviare, only I cannot eat them. There is cheese, and some ham which is not like any ham that I have ever known, and there is a sort of schnitzel sausage and some apples.

The soldier who was with us yesterday and is still with us, and whose name is Marinashky, is a chauffeur. I thought he was an officer. He eats with us, smokes with us, joins in the discussions and kindly lays the table for food and clears away for us. It sounds odd, but it seemed quite natural until I heard that he was a chauffeur. My bourgeois bringing-up is constantly having surprises! Marinashky has a nice clear-cut face, and square jaw like the Americans one saw during the war.

This afternoon we got out of the train and walked up the line, as there were three hours to dispose of. I led the way because there was a wood I wanted to go to. It was extremely pretty, and the moss sank beneath one's feet. The children collected berries and scarlet mushrooms, which they brought to me as offerings.

On the way back Kameneff and his boy and I found a dry place covered with pine needles, where we lay down, and to the sound of father and son talking softly in Russian I went fast asleep. The sun was setting when they woke me up. In the heart of Russia, in the company of Bolsheviks, I had spent an Arcadian hour.

SEPTEMBER 20TH. *Moscow, The Kremlin.*

Yesterday evening after we had started, Kameneff left us to go and talk to Zinoviev who was on the Petrograd train, travelling also to Moscow. Zinoviev is President of the Petrograd Soviet (and also of the Third International). I did not see Kameneff again that evening, but at 2 a.m. he knocked at my door and awakened me with many apologies to tell me news he thought I should like to hear. Zinoviev had just told him that the telegram announcing his arrival with me came in the middle of a Soviet Conference. It caused a good deal of amusement, but Lenin said that whatever one felt about it there was nothing to do but to give me some sittings as I had come so far for the purpose. 'So Lenin has consented and I thought it was worth while to wake you up to tell you that.' Kameneff was in great spirits; Zinoviev had evidently told him things he was glad to hear, especially, I gathered, that no blame or censure was going to be put upon him for having failed in his mission to England.

We reached Moscow at 10.30 a.m. and I waited in the train so that Kameneff and his wife could get their tender greetings over without my presence. I watched them through the window: the greeting on one side, however, was not apparent in its tenderness. I waited and they walked up the platform talking with animation. Finally Mrs. Kameneff came into the compartment and shook hands with me. Mrs. Philip Snowden in her book has described her as 'an amiable little lady'. She has small brown eyes and thin lips. She looked at the remains of our breakfast on the saloon table and said querulously, 'We don't live *chic* like that in Moscow.' Goodness, I thought, not even like that! There was more discussion in Russian between the two, and my expressionless face watched them. I have become reconciled to not being unable to understand.

As we left the train she said to me: 'Leo Kameneff has quite forgotten about Russia, the people here will say he is a bourgeois.' Leo Kameneff spat upon the platform in the most plebeian way, I suppose to disprove this. It was extremely unlike him.

We piled into a beautiful open Rolls-Royce car and were driven at full speed with a great deal of hooting through streets that were shuttered as after an air raid. Mrs. Kameneff said to me: 'It is dirty, our Moscow, isn't it?' Well, yes, one could not very well say that it was not.

We came to the Kremlin. It is high up and dominates Moscow and consists of the main palace, some other palaces, convents, monasteries, and churches encircled by a wall and towers. The sun was shining when we arrived and all the gold domes were glittering in the light. Everywhere one looked there were domes and towers.

We drove up to a side entrance under an archway, and then made our way, a solemn procession, carrying luggage up endless stone stairs and along stone corridors to the Kameneff apartments. A little peasant maid with a yellow handkerchief tied over her head ran out to greet us, and kissed Kameneff on the mouth. Then ensued the awkward moment of being shown to no room. After eleven days travelling one felt a longing for peace, and to be able to unpack, instead of which the Russian discussion was resumed, and I sat stupidly still with nothing to say.

For breakfast I was given coffee and an over-helping of dry tepid rice. When for a moment I found myself alone with Kameneff I asked him what was to become of me

MARINASHKY AND THE MINISTERIAL ROLLS-ROYCE

and begged him to send me to an hotel. But there are no hotels; everything belongs to the Government. There are, however, guest-houses, but he was averse to my going to one, as he said that I should be lonely and strange. He told me to leave the matter entirely to him and he would decide in two hours.

Meanwhile I went for a walk in the Kremlin grounds with Alexandre and took a lot of photographs. The beauty of it all was a wonderment, and I was quite happy not to go outside the walls, which I could not do as I had no pass. Then I came back and waited and waited for Kameneff to come and tell me where I was to go. As the day passed by I felt more and more lonely. For lack of another book I read de Maupassant's *Yvette*, but hated it, and thanked God that Bolshevism had at least wiped out that vile world of idle men. At sunset I sat on the ledge of the open window, and listened to the bells that were ringing from all the domes in Moscow. Below me was an avenue of trees that reached up to me with autumn colours. I thought of Dick and that today is his birthday. I knew he must be asking, 'Where is "Meema"; why doesn't she come? How long will she be?'

When it was dark I was still looking out, and Anna Anrevna, the little maid, came in softly in her string soled shoes and put her arms round me. She told me in broken German that I must not *traurig sein*.

Kameneff came in at half-past ten, he was very tired and precluded all further discussion by saying that it was too late to go anywhere else, and that I must stay for the night. Mrs. Kameneff came in from her work a little later. She sank into a chair and drew her hand across her brow in the most approved way to betoken physical exhaustion. I was given Alexandre's room,

SERGE TROTSKY AND ALEXANDRE KAMENEFF

through which they have to pass to get to theirs, and I have to pass through theirs to get to the wash-room, as there is no washstand in my bedroom. I suppose Alexandre slept on a sofa. Kameneff went back to his Soviet meeting at eleven, and I heard him pass through my room when he came home at 4 a.m.

SEPTEMBER 21ST.

I awakened, feeling much better. The sunshine was too wonderful. Both the Kameneffs went off to their respective work, she at 10, and he at 11. I went out into the Kremlin grounds with Alexandre, and while he played football with Serge Trotsky I sat among the columns of the Alexander Memorial and indulged in a kaleidoscope of thought. Serge is the twelve year old son of Trotsky, and is a fine little boy with a broad chest and a straight back. He looks like the heir to a throne in the guise of a peasant.

At 1 o'clock a cousin of Leo Kameneff's who can speak French and English came to fetch me. Outside the Kremlin gate an old man, who looked like a peasant, stopped me and asked in English if I were Sylvia Pankhurst.

Hearing I was not he asked: 'But you are English and I hope a good Communist?' I did not answer, I just pressed his hand.

We went to the Musée Alexandre III, the garden of which is strewn with large bronze eagles thrown down from the pediment. They are very emblematic of the mighty who are fallen.

The Museum contains replicas of classics of which the originals are in many cases in the British Museum. But the arrangement and the backgrounds are so good, that it gives one more pleasure to look at the Greek and

BRONZE EAGLE AT THE MUSÉE ALEXANDRE III

Assyrian replicas here than to see the originals in London.

A school of boys and girls, extremely well fed and well dressed, was being shown round, and there was also a magnificent old peasant with long hair and aquiline nose, who told us that he wanted before he died to see what a museum was like. Both he and the schoolmaster asked us if we could explain things to them as there were no guides. Even had I been able to speak the language, I should have been at a loss to explain the Parthenon Temple which we were facing at that moment. The children probably, and the peasant surely, had never heard of the Parthenon, nor of Greek mythology; where would one begin? One could only have said: 'Isn't it beautiful, don't you see how beautiful it is?' and hope that they did see it. Since I heard a guide explaining Rodin at South Kensington to Australian soldiers, I have felt sure that Art can be felt, but not explained.

In the end we procured a guidebook and sent the old peasant off with the children's school, and left the master to do his best. When I got back it was to find no one at home. I ate some food, as I was hungry, and concluded that I was still to be a guest at the Kremlin. Late in the afternoon I found my way alone through the maze of corridors and staircases, out into the grounds alone. I wandered about, still hypnotised by the beauty of the sun-reflecting domes, and by the dead stillness which seemed to protest from the Royal stones. Over the Tsar's palace crows pecked at the flagstaff where once the Royal Standard had flown. There is a clock in a tower at the Kremlin Gate and it has a complaining and depressing chime. It complains once at the quarter, four times at the hour. It seemed to say, 'My people are gone! and

I am sad, and I am sad.' It doubtless complained when Napoleon took possession, and again in Tsarist days, and probably will always lament; some people are never satisfied.

I have a sort of feeling that I am staying at Versailles just after Louis XVI. My emotions and impressions are too deep, too many, and too bewildering to be measured in words.

In the evening Alexandre took me to a play at the Théâtre des Arts. A big theatre and well filled. The piece was very well staged. The play, which is adapted from an old Polish legend called 'Corrodine', was well acted, so that without understanding a word I gathered some of the sense. In front of us sat Madame Zinoviev with a Comrade and I was glad when they talked to me in French. It was not until afterwards that I learnt who she was, much to my amusement, remembering that I had told her my errand, and that Zinoviev was among the heads promised to me. She asked me if I would not have to go to Petrograd to do him, but I said that I thought not, as he was in Moscow at the moment, and that if I could only find a place to work in, he would sit to me at once. I wondered why she laughed.

SEPTEMBER 22ND. *Moscow, The Guest House.*

Mrs. Kameneff went to her work as usual at 10 a.m. At breakfast half an hour later Leo Borisvitch, as he is called, promised not to do any work or keep any engagement until he had taken me to my new headquarters in a guest-house. We were delayed in starting by John Reed, the American Communist, who came to see him on some business. He is a well-built good-looking young man, who has given up everything at home to throw his heart and life into work here. I understand the *Russian* spirit, but what strange force impels an apparently normal young man from the United States? There also arrived to waylay us a painter called Rosenfeld, who wore canvas shoes like a peasant, and kissed Kameneff on his arrival. He offered to show me museums and things, but our only medium was German, and his was a good deal worse than mine, which was a great drawback. At midday, however, we broke free, and started off with my luggage. I bade farewell to the Kremlin, and we drove across the river to a guest-house on the opposite bank facing the Tsar's Palace. The guest-house is the requisitioned house of a sugar king. It is inhabited by various Foreign Office officials, also by Mr. Rothstein and an American financier, Mr. W. B. Vanderlip. A beautiful bedroom and dressing-room are mine, with walls of green damask. It looks more like a drawing-room than a bedroom. The house is more or less exactly as the sugar king left it, full of a mixture of good and bad things. It is partly modern Gothic and partly German Louis XVI. The ceiling of one of the big rooms is painted by Flameng, but the best pictures (there were some Corots) have been taken to a museum. One is extremely grateful for its comfort and hospitality, even if its taste in decoration is not of the best.

Moreover, one can enjoy it light-headedly, for the exiled sugar king, it is rumoured, had other palaces abroad, and never came to Moscow except for a few weeks in the year. He also has money invested abroad and is not in want, and can well spare his Moscow palace for so good a purpose. His old manservant waits upon us, and takes the tenderest care of the house in the belief that the old regime will return, bringing the owners of

ROTHSTEIN, SHOWING THE KREMLIN IN THE BACKGROUND

the house with it. He says openly that he is not a Bolshevik, and takes much pride in changing our plates a great many times, and making the most of our humble fare. He insists that so far as it depends upon him we shall behave like perfect ladies and gentlemen and be treated as such.

I stayed at home all day unpacking at last, and settling down into my temporary home. Kameneff promised to come back in the course of the day, but he didn't. He telephoned however, and arranged that I should be taken to the Ballet with the party from this house. We sat in the Foreign Office box. The ballet was *Coppelia*, beautifully produced, and the orchestra one of the finest that I ever heard. The theatre is the size of Covent Garden, and is decorated with crimson and gold. There are boxes all round the first tier, and the house was packed throughout.

The audience consisted of working people, who had admission free through the distribution of tickets to certain unions. They were a motley crowd, chiefly *en blouse*. In the Royal box, reserved for Commissars and their wives, there was a man with a cloth cap. The women were eating apples. In the box next to ours there was an old woman with a shawl over her head.

It was intensely moving to see the absorbed attention of the audience. People leaned their elbows on the ledges of the boxes and watched the ballet with an almost devouring interest. There was not a cough nor a whisper. Only when Coppelia came to life as the mechanical doll, there were delicious low ripples of controlled laughter from the children. At the ends of the acts people left the stalls to rush, not for the exits to the foyer, but to the front of the gangways nearest the stage to see the dancers close to, and to applaud them. The people were tired people, who had worked all day and had earned a good evening and were enjoying it to the full.

My only contretemps was with a little stenographer from the Foreign Office who was in our box. She observed that I had on the red enamelled star of Communism, and that I wore white gloves. One, she said, contradicted the other; the white gloves were bourgeois. I argued that it only mattered what was in my heart, and not what was on my hands. But she would not be pacified, so I removed the gloves. Considering that my costume was a red tweed skirt with a red wool jersey and a tight-fitting cap, I had thought that gloves would not make me over-dressed.

If my evening's pleasure was neutralised by the con-centrated aroma which arose from the great unwashed, it is only fair to observe that there is no soap in the country, and most people have, for two years or so, only had the one suit of clothes in which they stand up. No wonder—! In the car coming home I met Mr. Rothstein, who is living in the same house. I wished I could recall the abusive article which I read about him in an English newspaper, but all I remember is that he is not to be readmitted to England. He seems to be an energetic and forceful little man. I expect he is pretty clever. We had supper together after the theatre, and conversation drifted on to that eternal comedy, the Nationalisation of women. I happened to say that this had done more to harm the Bolshevik cause than almost anything, and, moreover, that quite serious people still believed it. Mr. Rothstein interposed rather sharply, 'Well, a little select circle which reads the *Morning Post* perhaps believes it.'

Is it possible, I wonder, that he is right, and that the

'little select circle' do not count as much as I have all my life taken for granted that they did?

SEPTEMBER 23RD.

I wasted a lot of time this morning trying to fix things up without the help of Kameneff. As things have turned out I might have saved myself the trouble. John Reed told me that I never would begin work unless I arranged everything for myself, and depended on no one here. On the other hand Mr. Vanderlip told me to keep calm, as his experience was that everything came in time. Thoroughly impatient, however, I got hold of Mr. Rosenfeld who arrived simultaneously with Alexandre Kameneff and a motor. Rosenfeld took me studio hunting. The Art Schools seemed to be very far away from the parts of Moscow that are familiar to me, and although everyone was willing to help, there seemed to be little accommodation available. In the Academia, which I believe is only just re-opening, they offered me a place to work in – a gallery which obviously was not suitable. We went on to the Strogonoff School, where Mr. Konenkoff, one of their most distinguished sculptors, offered me of his best. It was like an empty kitchen looking into a bleak courtyard. The two students who followed us round were not very sympathetic. No doubt they thought it presumptuous of me to come to Russia and expect to model Lenin! They certainly did not seem to think he would sit to me. Kameneff had warned me that most of the artists I should meet would not be Bolsheviks, so that probably the students I met were not, but thought that I was. One of them, a girl and more friendly than the rest, said to me in French: 'If you are a friend of those in power I suppose you will get some food; we are expected to work here all day from 9 in the morning till 6 at night without any.' I asked why she did not bring her food with her, and received some jumbled explanation about rations and distribution and State Control and no shops, which was so bewildering that I avoided further discussion. It was obvious that I did not understand the condition of things, and that I looked rather stupid in consequence. Another one said to me: 'Madame, we are waiting for deliverance. For two years we have waited. We do not know how it is to come, but we just hope that some morning we may wake up to find the nightmare over.' I said feebly that there had been six years of war, and a blockade, but I felt it was no business of mine to put up a defence for their system. I came home thoroughly depressed and disheartened, having accomplished nothing. At 10 p.m. I was sitting in the gilded drawing-room with Mr. Vanderlip when the telephone rang: it was Kameneff. He announced that he had a room for me at the Kremlin and that I must work there because all the people I had to model were there, and that it was the only way to get them as they were very busy. He promised to send someone for me in the morning to take me there. He asked if I were lonely, resentful, or bored, and pleaded his inability to get to me owing to stress of work. He begged me to be patient and good, and promised that all would come right. I went to bed feeling really better.

SEPTEMBER 24TH.

Madame Kameneff's secretary fetched me at 10 a.m. and we found a Comrade waiting for us at the Kremlin gateway. He was a painter, young and bearded, who could speak only Russian. We got our passes to get into

BIG GUN AT THE KREMLIN

BIG BELL, KREMLIN

the big round building which used to be the Courts of Justice, and where the conferences are now held. It is the chief building, and the Red flag flies above it. Once inside we walked for ever as it seemed, along stone corridors full of busy people. We went to the room of Comrade Unachidse, one of the most magnificent men that I have ever seen, a real Mestrovic type, strong features and bushy red hair. Unfortunately he also could only speak Russian. He showed me the room which is placed at my disposal. It is big and nearly empty, semi-circular in shape, with bare white-washed walls. In one corner a formidable iron door with round peep-holes in it leads into a small cell which contains a safe. The safe is sealed up with Soviet seals. The cell, I was told, was a disused prison. This probably accounted for the atmos-phere of depression and grimness which persisted in spite of the sunlight which in the afternoon flooded my three big windows. Opposite, across the courtyard, is the Arsenal, and all along the Arsenal walls are ranged the masses of cannon with their 'N' surrounded by the laurel wreath, which leaves one in no doubt as to their origin.

While I was looking round, Kameneff turned up; he told me to make a list of my requirements, and then carried me off in a car and was able to stay with me until 2 o'clock. These moments together snatched in between work are so rare that one almost values them. He told me I was to go to a meeting at the theatre in the evening, and promised that I should be in a box near the stage so that I could see well. He was to address the meeting on the subject of his visit to England.

The party from our house were late in starting. We got to the theatre after the meeting had begun, and were put in the Tsar's box. This was already crammed full to overflowing, and all the chairs were occupied by Turks, Chinese and Persians. No one attempted to offer me a place. Mr. Vanderlip and I stood for some time, while people moved in and out and Turks and Persians (I shall never want to smell geranium again) pushed us about in their impatient efforts to get past or over us. All my British blood was boiling, and I realised that for the time being, at all events, I could not regard the Turks and Persians and Chinese as my brothers.

After a while Mr. Vanderlip and I were moved to the stage box. This too was full, but not of the same kind of people. Anyway, it was nearer, and one got a better view. Clara Zetkin, the German Socialist, was speaking, spitting forth venom, as it sounded. The German language is not beautiful, and the ferocious old soul, mopping her plain face with a large handkerchief, was not inspiring. It sounded very hysterical and I only understood an outline of what she was saying. Then Trotsky got up, and translated her speech into Russian. He interested me very much. He is a man with a slim, good figure, splendid fighting countenance, and his whole personality is full of force. I look forward immensely to doing his head. There is something that ought to lend itself to a fine piece of work. The overcrowded house was as still as if it were empty, everyone was attentive and concentrated.

After Trotsky Mme. Kolontai spoke. She has short dark hair. Perhaps she spoke well, but of that I could not judge. Tired of standing and of not understanding I left the theatre at the moment when a great many repetitions of Churchill's and Lloyd George's names were rocking the house with laughter.

SEPTEMBER 25TH.

I feel very discouraged. Everyone I meet asks me what I have come to Moscow for. They assure me that there is no chance of modelling Lenin, and still less of doing Dzhirjinsky, who is a recluse. Nevertheless, I have spent the day getting everything in order. Sackfuls of bone-dry clay have been delivered at my door. Five men and one girl stood inert and watched me break it up with a crow-bar. Finally I was able to send them all away except one, a really intelligent carpenter, who, instead of trying to talk to me, watched me and understood what I wanted. He was splendid, made three armatures for me, and then beat and stirred the clay for three hours until it was in condition. When Kameneff looked in, bringing Zinoviev, I was up to my elbows in clay, my clothes were covered and my hair was standing on end. Zinoviev laughed, and said it was obvious that I should not be ready for him to sit to me for days, but I assured him all would be in order tomorrow, and added that a man of the carpenter's intelligence was worthy to be a Government minister. Kameneff repeated this to the carpenter, and then said to me: 'Here everything is possible.' Before leaving he gave me a pass into the Kremlin that will last until December, so I am independent at last, and can go in and out alone when I please. I did not come home until I had built up two heads ready to work on. I am very tired but full of hope, remembering that I have heard that things come slowly in Russia, but they come eventually.

SEPTEMBER 26TH.

I went to church at St. Saviour's, the big church beyond the bridge, which was built with the private

ST. SAVIOUR'S

money of the Tsar as a thanksgiving for deliverance from Napoleon. It has five gold domes which are a beacon to me when I am lost. A service was going on and we mingled with the crowd, which had an amazing preponderance of men. The richness of the church with its golden and crimson robed priests seemed to throw into relief the poverty of the people with their faces so full of sadness. What absurdly stupid things animate one's thoughts in the most precious moments: for instance, when the priest made the sign of the Cross with the three branched candlesticks in each hand, I instinctively looked to see if he had dropped candle-grease on the carpet – he had! When the contribution plate began to circulate I watched an old peasant next to me. He drew out his pocket-book, and fumbled for a few roubles. He held five of these like a card-hand and fingered them hesitatingly. It was obvious that he was trying to make up his mind whether he could afford to part with them all, or only with some of them. In the end he put them all into the plate, a little act of sacrifice, which I am sure will not pass unblessed.

The choir singing without accompaniment was very beautiful. The masses seemed to be very fervent, one could see Faith and Hope in all their faces. It is surely the deep religious feeling in Russia that has sustained these people through all their years of privation, and prevented a greater chaos.

After church we walked along, rejoicing in the sun, to the Tretiakovskaya Gallery, full of various schools of painting. Among the pictures is the famous one of Ivan the Terrible killing his son, but everything that I saw was obliterated by the memory of three modern busts, the work of Konenoff, the sculptor I met at the Strogonoff

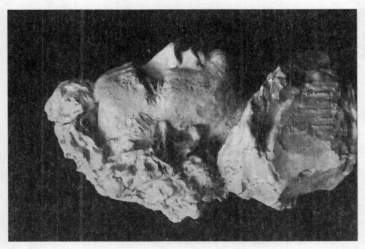

BUST OF ZINOVIEV

School. These busts are carved out of blocks of wood. They are indescribable masterpieces in conception, composition and carving. I remained for some time in admiration and wonderment over this modern work, and then went away, as I could not look at anything else.

At 3 o'clock I hurried to the Kremlin, as Kameneff had telephoned telling me to expect Zinoviev. I waited until four and then he arrived, busy, tired and impatient, his overcoat slung over his shoulders as though he had not had time to put his arms through the sleeves. He slung off his hat and ran his fingers through his black curly hair, which already was standing on end. He sat restlessly looking up and down, round and out and beyond; then he read his newspaper, every now and again flashing round with an imperative look at me to see how I was getting on. He seemed to me an extraordinary mix-up of conflicting personalities. He has the eyes and brow of the fighting man, and the mouth of a petulant woman.

Little by little he became more tractable, and when he had finished reading we talked a little. At moments he threw his head back and seemed to be dreaming. Then he looked like a poet. He is only thirty-eight. It is amazing how young all these Revolutionaries are. I gleaned from him the news that Millerand is the new President of the French, to which he shrugged his shoulders and said that it made no difference, and that the British strike fixed for tomorrow has been postponed for a week. Before he left he said he was pleased with the start of his bust, and that I must do Lenin.

I walked home in face of a lovely sunset; the fiery ball was reflected in the gold dome of St. Saviour's. I sang as I walked, because I have begun work at last, but people looked at me, although they had never looked at me before. I suppose it was peculiar to hear anyone sing.

SEPTEMBER 27TH.

Things begin to move more rapidly now, and my patience is being rewarded. Today Dzhirjinsky came. He is the President of the Extraordinary Commission, or as we should call it in English, the organiser of the Red Terror. He is the man Kameneff has told me so much about. He sat for an hour and a half, quite still and very silent. His eyes certainly looked as if they were bathed in tears of eternal sorrow, but his mouth smiled an indulgent kindness. His face is narrow, with high cheek bones and sunk in. Of all his features his nose seems to have the most character. It is very refined, and the delicate bloodless nostrils suggest the sensitiveness of over-breeding. He is a Pole by origin.

As I worked and watched him during that hour and a half he made a curious impression on me. Finally, overwhelmed by his quietude, I exclaimed : 'You are an angel to sit so still.' Our medium was German, which made fluent conversation between us impossible, but he answered: 'One learns patience and calm in prison.'

I asked how long he was in prison. 'A quarter of my life, eleven years,' he answered. It was the Revolution that liberated him. Obviously it is not the abstract desire for power or for a political career that has made Revolutionaries of such men, but a fanatical conviction of the wrongs to be righted for the cause of humanity and national progress. For this cause men of sensitive intellect have endured years of imprisonment.

Being Monday there is no theatre, as that is the night the artists have free – on Sundays they work for the enjoyment of the people – so I dined with Mr. Vanderlip, who told me many things which I may not at this juncture write down or repeat. I have not sought his confidence, so I thought it rather unjustifiable when at the end of the evening, having found me a sympathetic listener, he said: 'You know too much now, I shall see that you do not leave the country before I do.' Although he likes the people with whom he has come in business contact, he is frankly a capitalist, and glories in it. He is like the Englishman abroad who is conscious of being different to everyone else, and derives from it a smug feeling of superiority.

After dinner he was sent for by Tchicherin, and I spent the evening with Michael Borodin. Michael Markovitch, as Borodin is called, lives in our house. He is a man with shaggy black hair brushed back from his forehead, a Napoleonic beard, deep-set eyes, and a face like a mask. He talks abrupt American-English in a base voice. I have not seen much of him as he works half the day and all the night, like the other Foreign Office officials. He is usually late for meals, eats hurriedly and leaves before we have finished. As soon as Vanderlip had gone Borodin switched out all the drawing-room lights that Vanderlip had put on, except one. I asked him why he did this, and he looked round the garish room and gave a slight shudder: 'It is parvenu,' he said; then sinking back into his chair he looked at me intently, and asked: 'What is your economic position in the world?' It is the first time he has talked to me, and I found myself answering as if my life depended on my answers. Happily no one in this country knows anything about my family, up-bringing, or surroundings. I have not got to live down my wasted years. I can stand on my own feet and be accepted on my

BUST OF DZHIRJINSKY

own merits. Borodin mystifies me, I cannot make out, when all his questions have been answered, what he thinks.

SEPTEMBER 28TH.

Dzhirjinsky came at 10 a.m. for an hour. He is leaving Moscow for a fortnight, so that I can get no more sittings, but seeing how keen I was, he stayed on and on, doling out ten minutes and quarter-hours as so much fine gold. He sits so well that two sittings are worth four of Zinoviev's.

When the Savonarola of the Revolution left, I felt a real sadness that I may never see him again. Zinoviev sat again in the afternoon, and brought with him Bucharin and Bela Kun. They seemed to approve of Dzhirjinsky's bust, and insisted on looking through all the photographs of my work. The 'Victory' is what really interests them.

I was frightfully disappointed in Bela Kun. I had imagined a romantic figure, but he looks most disreputable. Bucharin is attractive with his trim, neat little beard and young face.

This afternoon, after all had left, three soldiers brought a gilt Louis XVI sofa and a Turkestan carpet to my workroom. These had been ordered to help to make it more habitable and to dispel the severity. I had to laugh, the sofa looked so absurdly refined and out of place. I wondered whose drawing-room it once furnished, and to what little tea-time gossips it had listened. At that moment a sculptor called Nicholas Andrev came in and introduced himself to me. He was sent by Kameneff and mercifully speaks French. A big man with small laughing eyes and a red-grey beard,

NICHOLAS ANDREV

typically Russian. After we had talked for a while he described to me the difficulties under which he had tried to do Lenin in his office, and while he was working. He said that portraiture was not Art. I could not but agree with him, as the difficulty always in doing portraits is that sittings are always too few and too short, but said that one had to put up with it, and do the best one could, breaking one's heart over it all the time.

He said he had given up sculpture for the time being because of the difficult conditions, and had taken to drawing instead. I said that for the present I was intent on portraits, and that Art would have to wait until later. His attitude is characteristic of the sculptor species. They are all so d——d proud, and if they cannot get all the sittings they need and work under ideal conditions, they do not think it worth while trying. I consider that there are a few people in the world who are worth any effort to do, even if they do not give one a chance to do one's best work. Andrev laughed and said that that was journalism in Art.

When I got home I found that the water had been heated for baths. This was a great joy as I had not had one for eight days. Once a week is our allowance, and it should be on Saturdays, but something went wrong with the pipe, and we have been disappointed each evening, so that in fact I had given up hope. How one has learned to appreciate the most ordinary things that one never thought of being thankful for before. But since I have been here I have had to wash in cold water; nor am I called, but I wake up quite mechanically every morning at eight. It will be wonderful to have scrambled eggs one day for breakfast, but I am getting used to just black bread and butter, and sometimes cheese.

I wonder a good deal about my family and friends. It is so strange to have left them without a word, and to get no letters and not to be able to write any. Mamma especially – bless her, who always says 'good-night' as if it were 'goodbye-for-ever' – I wonder what she feels about my going off without telling her. I wonder if Papa is anxious about me, or indifferent and resentful! When I think about Dick and Margaret I feel a sadness. I can get on without most people in the world, but not without those two, and they must wonder why they do not get letters from me. It is rather dreadful to think that they might believe that my silence means forgetfulness.

This evening we went to the 'Coq d'Or'. I thought I was back in London until I looked away from the stage.

SEPTEMBER 30TH.

Kameneff came to see me in the morning with his watch in his hand, he had twenty minutes. It was paralysing, one cannot talk under such conditions. I confined myself to presenting him with a list of things I want done! Small wonder he comes so seldom to see me. When he does come everyone in the house knows it, and one by one they come to my door and ask to see him, each wanting something of him, while his car which waits at the door is borrowed for an errand. It is very discouraging for him.

Borodin took me to *Prince Igor* this evening, it combined the opera with the ballet. In the box next to us was a party of Afghans and with them a Korean. Down in the stalls *one* man was in a smoking coat and evening shirt, the first I have seen. He was very conspicuous.

79

OCTOBER 1ST.

Nicholas Andrev met me at the Kremlin at 1 o'clock. Kameneff had placed a car at our disposal for the afternoon. We went to several galleries, beginning with the Kremlin. The palace of a Grand Duchess (opposite the big bell) has been converted into a working people's club. It was quite clean and cared for, but only the Empire Swan furniture suggested it had ever been a private habitation. We went downstairs to a private chapel, painted in black and gold. This had been made into a modelling school, and there were some very good things being done from life. The Spirit of the Holy Ghost descending as a dove from above, and the golden rays of a carved sun made a strange background. My bourgeois prejudice was just for a moment shocked, until I remembered that in our own old fourteenth century chapel at home Papa typewrites on the altar step. It has been longer in disuse it is true, but still, one must be consistent. From there we drove in the car to the house of Ostrouckof, who showed me his room full of Ikons, one of which came out of St. Sofia. Some date back to the fifth and sixth centuries. They were beautiful in design and colour, and most interesting when he explained them to me. Downstairs he had a modern motley collection. He showed us a Mattisse given to him by Mattisse himself; it was a curious contrast after Ikons.

We drifted into some art schools, where soldiers and sailors were working from life models, and the work they were doing was extremely good. One of these schools was in the large house of a rich merchant. The Soviet Government are pretty shrewd in the selection of houses for various purposes. Although some of the big houses are places, often given over for clubs or workplaces, only a really vulgar, over-decorated house in impossibly bad taste is used for rough or dirty work.

The exhibitions of proletarian art are very interesting, and deeply imbued with the modern movement. There are crude drawings that show an appreciation of form, and there is sculpture in wood that is often very effective, and may lead to something good.

One of these exhibitions was in an exquisite house of beautiful architecture that stood back from the street, in a garden that had run to seed. The house had once belonged to the Princess Dolgorouki, but had been passed into the hands of a Countess somebody, who had died. The daughter *héritière* had been turned out, but it was said that she was still living in the basement. The ground floor consisted of a series of small, beautifully proportioned rooms, with painted ceilings and carved doors. One was a Chinese room and all were in exquisite taste. There were some lovely Empire bronzes and old Dorée, and other objects of art.

The house seemed to be open to anyone who chose to come in. The old cherry-satin upholstery of the French chairs was in limbo. I never felt a place so small and full of ghosts. Perhaps, because it was so small, it had the feeling of having been someone's intimate home, not a blatant place of entertaining.

As we wandered round a man joined us and, speaking to us in French, asked if we were from France. His cap was drawn well over his eyes, and the collar of his overcoat turned up over his ears. One could only see a well-bred nose pinched with cold. He knew about the house and its history, and which were the best bits of furniture. He was evidently a cultured man, and but for the presence of Andrev, who always laughs at me, I would have talked to him about himself. He was rather like a ghost haunting a place he knew, and I imagine he was not a Bolshevik , but one who had known prosperous days.

I came away filled with sadness, and when Kameneff came to see me this evening, I tried to tell him about it, and begged him to have the house taken care of. He says that there is a committee that looks after all the houses, but I think they have passed this one by.

Coming back from our wanderings we passed, in one of the squares, a statue of Gogol, the Russian writer. I thought it a very fine piece of work. Gogol, half wrapped in a cloak, looks down scrutinisingly in bronze from his rough granite seat, and Andrev laughed at me for liking it, and said that in Moscow it was scorned and had brought coals of fire down on the artist's head.

I was very surprised, and thought to myself that the standard of Russian art must be very high: but in spite of this ridicule, I stuck to my opinion. I even said that in London we had not a single statue as good as that one. Later he admitted that he was the author of it.

OCTOBER 2ND.

Hearing that there was a review of troops in the Red Square at 11 o'clock, I went to see what I could see. Everyone else seemed busy, and Michael Markovitch, whom I wanted, was not to be found. If he had come with me I should have taken my kodak, but I have not a permit and did not feel like risking a controversy alone. Arrived in the Red Square, I was not allowed to get anywhere near, and I did so want to see and hear Trotsky addressing the troops. Soldiers kept the onlookers absolutely out of the square, and I stood on the steps of the

CHURCH OF ST. BASIL

wonderful church of St. Basil. The soldiers certainly were very amiable, and, when I wandered rebelliously from my steps out into the road, a bayonet was levelled smilingly at me; I made a gesture of not understanding, and said helplessly in English 'Where do you want me to go?' Whereupon the soldier laughed and allowed me to stand by his side. The crowd was very quiet and apathetic, one certainly was not near enough to get excited. In the dim distance one could hear Trotsky's voice, punctuated by cheers from the soldiers. After a while the crowd broke forward to where I stood with the soldier. Some mounted detachments came towards us, very decorative indeed with bright coloured uniforms and lances with fluttering pennons. Suddenly a man at my side said to me in French: 'Madame, does this please you?' I was very glad to have someone to speak to; the man was young, and, though ill-shaved, was well-dressed in uniform. He could speak German also, but English he said he had forgotten, though he had at one time spent three months in England. Waving a hand contemptuously towards the scene before us, he said: *C'est du théâtre, Madame* – that is all it amounts to.' I ventured to say that a theatrical display was not much use unless there were spectators. In England, I assured him, we had our military pageants for the benefit of the people, but what was the use of this if we were not allowed anywhere near? He replied that it was a necessary precaution for the protection of Trotsky. I laughed: 'We are three gunshots away, at least.' Then to my amazement the man began to discuss and criticise, and talk what seemed to me pure Counter-Revolutionary stuff. From all one has ever heard about Russian conditions (Tsarist as well as Revolutionary) it seemed to me that he was strangely indiscreet, and I asked him: 'Are you not mad to talk like this in a crowd? Anyone may understand French.' He shrugged his shoulders: 'One has lived so long now side by side with death that one has grown callous.' He then asked if I would care to go for a walk. I felt rather self-conscious of walking away in front of the crowd with a man whom they had seen me so obviously 'pick up'. However, in Russia there are no conventions, it was only my bourgeois blood rushing to the surface again that made it seem peculiar.

We went down to the river and leaned against the railing and talked for a long time. He was certainly very interesting and amazingly indiscreet. Happily I have nothing with which to reproach myself. I adopted a perfectly good Bolshevik point of view, and argued in my usual way about wars and blockades, and urged him to have imagination and to look further ahead than today and tomorrow. We talked about idealists, reviewed a few Tsarist items, and made comparisons, but everything I said provoked him to further extreme utterances. He wished finally that he might have an opportunity of showing me 'the other side'. He invited me to go to a factory with him. I asked what use that would be as I cannot speak a word of Russian. He said he would like to present to me his father and his uncle, but as they were both 'known' he would have to be very careful. Finally we exchanged my name and address for his telephone number. He said that if I would telephone him tomorrow, Sunday night, he would meet me outside my front gate at 11 on Monday morning, but he would not dare to come into the house.

At 1 o'clock a.m. (I have adopted the Russian habit of not going to bed) I saw Michael Markovitch, when he returned from the Commissariat, and told him about it. He said that he must be the queerest sort of Counter-Revolutionary he had ever heard of, and advised me to leave him alone.

OCTOBER 3RD.

I have been five days out of work. It seems much longer. I am told that there are people in Moscow who have been waiting six months to accomplish the business they came for. Lenin seems to me further away than he did in London. There is nothing to do here unless one has work. Never could one have imagined a world in which there is absolutely no social life and no shops. There are no newspapers (for me) and no letters, either to be received or written. There are no meals to look forward to, and comfort cannot be sought in a hot bath. When one has seen all the galleries, and they are open only half a day, and some of them not every day, and when one has walked over cobblestones until one's feet ache, there is nothing more to be done. One must have work to do. Perhaps I should be calmer if I had already accomplished Lenin, but my anxiety is lest I should have to wait weary weeks. Return to London without his head I cannot. Michael took me for a walk, and it was extremely cold. We went to St. Basil, as I wanted to see it inside, but it is locked after 3 o'clock. Outside it is wonderful, painted all over in various designs and colours. I cannot understand how it stands the climate. Inside I am told that there is not much to see; Napoleon stabled his horses in it. One has heard so much about Bolshevik outrages, but they have done nothing like that. Napoleon distinguished himself in several ways while he was here. For instance, he ordered the destruc-

SPASSKY ENTRANCE TO THE KREMLIN

tion of the beautiful Spassky Gate of the Kremlin; the barrels of powder were placed in position and the matches were lit as the last of the French rode out. The Cossacks galloped up in time to put the matches out at the risk of their lives.

On our way home we passed by St. Saviour's church and looked in, really impelled to seek refuge from the cold. In a side chapel where the light was dim, a priest, with his long hair and beard and fine features, was preaching to a congregation which sat fervently absorbed. The heads of the women looked Eastern in their shawl swathings. I listened for some time to the strange musical tongue, of which I could not understand a word. The priest looked so amazingly like the traditional pictures of Christ that I felt I was listening to the great Master teaching in the Temple.

OCTOBER 4TH.

When I came down to breakfast at 10 my strange Counter-Revolutionary was sitting in the hall. How he ever got there or why he came as I had not telephoned to him, I shall never understand. I expressed my astonishment and told him I was sorry I could not go out with him, as I had someone coming to see me. I promised to telephone to him later. He seemed a little disappointed, said he was '*entièrement a mon service*', and departed. In the dining-room I found Michael breakfasting and told him, and he got up quickly to see, but I laughed and said that naturally I had sent him away, before telling anyone he was there. Michael looked at me with a cold look. He is like the others, one feels instinctively that however much they may like one as a woman, they would sacrifice one in a minute if it were necessary for the cause.

At lunch time H. G. Wells arrived from Petrograd with his son; they are lodged in our house. It was a great pleasure to find an old friend and to be able to talk of things and people familiar to us. He was, as usual, laughing and extremely humorous about the condition of life in Petrograd. On his account we were a big party for lunch, and there was an effort to make a spread, but this was frustrated by Michael Borodin. When I asked for some of the beautiful apple cake I had seen on the side-table, Michael made grimaces at me: he had sent it back to the kitchen. The perfect Communist in him revolted against the inequality of H. G. having a special cake, considering that neither Vanderlip nor Sheridan had had one on arrival. The household call me Sheridan, like a man. One has quite lost the habit of prefixing Mr. or Mrs., in fact one cannot do it, it sounds so absurd and affected. I have not yet been honoured to the extent of being called Tovarisch (Comrade), but some people call me Clara Moretonovna (Clare, daughter of Moreton).

After lunch I went for a walk with Michael; he had tip-toed out of the room at lunch time, and I asked him why. He was not very communicative, and said that he hated people collectively and he disliked H. G., though for no reason that I could make out. I sat up far into the night. One felt quite sleepless with excitement over the evening's discussions.

OCTOBER 5TH.

H. G. had an hour's interview with Lenin. He told me that he was impressed by the man, and liked him. Lenin apparently told him all about the Vanderlip business, the Kamschatka concessions and the Alliance against Japan. This will greatly upset Vanderlip, who did not want the news to leave the country until he did. But I expect Lenin's indiscretion is the indiscretion of purpose. H. G. talked to me at some length about the advisability of my going home. He, too, is discouraging about my prospects of doing Lenin or Trotsky. He says that Kameneff has 'let me down' badly. I could only say in Kameneff's defence that he has not 'let me down' yet. But H. G. had something else in the back of his head that he did not tell. I gathered that he thinks there will be trouble here in a few weeks. What the conditions are in Petrograd I do not know, but here one feels as safe as a mountain and as immovable. H. G. may learn a lot of facts about schools and factories and things, but it is only by living a life of dull routine and work, even of patient inactivity and waiting, that one absorbs the atmosphere. Inactivity is forced upon me, I *have* to wait. I am waiting neither patiently nor calmly it is true, but all the while I realise that I am gaining something, and that some understanding is subconsciously flowing to me. I see no danger signals. A winter of hardship and sacrifice for these people, yes, but no disorder. The machine is slowly, very slowly, working with more competence and freedom. Of course one dislikes cold baths in cold weather, and bad food, and all the discomforts to which a pampered life has made one unaccustomed, but these need not blight one's outlook. They are not necessarily indicative of a disruption.

After the Ballet *Sadko*, I walked home with Michael Borodin. We had supper together of cabbage-soup and tepid rice, and talked until 2 a.m. Michael always says that the food is eatable, even if it is not. He never complains, he just pretends to eat it, sometimes I see his pretence. This evening he talked to me about my work. He wants me to think about a statue interpreting the Soviet idea, and told me a good deal about the Third International, as representing a world brotherhood of workers. The plan of the Third International is very fine: 'Workmen of the world unite.' If they did unite they could hold the peace of the world for ever. But unity is hard to attain; I wonder if it is not unattainable. Everything that one hears and sees here stirs the imagination – my mind is seething with allegories with which to express them, but they are so big that I should have to settle for life on the side of a mountain, and hew out my allegories from the mountain side. Tonight, in his big Gothic room, I paced back and forth, my arm through Michael's, talking abstractedly, until his calmness calmed me. He knows that I have been going through a period of waiting, not unmixed with despair and anxiety. I understand so little about the Russian temperament, and hear such conflicting reports, that it is difficult to know what to expect. He has encouraged and cheered and tolerated me. He reminds me sometimes of Munthe,[1] in his adhesion to his convictions, and his demand that one should live up to one's idealism.

OCTOBER 6TH.

Spent the morning darning my stockings and reading Rupert Brooke. I was depressed to the point of resignation. It is always blackest before dawn: at 2 o'clock the Commandant of the house walked in with a telephone message: 'Greetings from Comrade Kameneff, and all is

1   Dr. Axel Munthe, San Michele, Anacapri, Italy.

91

prepared for you to go and do Lenin in his room tomorrow, from 11 till 4 o'clock.'

It was marvellous news. I went directly to the Kremlin, and with the help of someone from the Foreign Office, got my stands and clay moved from my studio to Lenin's room. I happily had him built up, ready to work on as soon as the order should come.

OCTOBER 7TH.

Borodin accompanied me to the Kremlin. On the way he said to me: 'Just remember that you are going to do the best bit of work today that you have ever done.' I was anxious, rather, about the conditions of the room and the light.

We went in by a special door, guarded by a sentry, and on the third floor we went through several doors and passages, each guarded. As I was expected, the sentries had received orders to let me pass. Finally, we went through two rooms full of women secretaries. The last room contained about five women at five tables, and they all looked at me curiously, but they knew my errand. Here Michael handed me over to a little hunchback, Lenin's private secretary, and left me. She pointed to a white baize door, and I went through. It did not latch, but merely swung behind me.

Lenin was sitting at his desk. He rose and came across the room to greet me. He has a genial manner and a kindly smile, which puts one instantly at ease. He said that he had heard of me from Kameneff. I apologised for having to bother him. He laughed and explained that the last sculptor had occupied his room for weeks, and that he got so bored with it that he had sworn that it never should happen again. He asked how long I needed, and offered me today and tomorrow from 11 till 4, and three or four evenings, if I could work by electric light. When I told him I worked quickly and should probably not require so much, he said laughingly that he was pleased.

My stand and things were then brought into the room by three soldiers, and I established myself on the left. It was hard work, for he was lower than the clay and did not revolve, nor did he keep still. But the room was so peaceful, and he on the whole took so little notice of me, that I worked with great calm till 3.45, without stopping for rest or food.

During that time he had but one interview, but the telephone was of great assistance to me. When the low buzz, accompanied by the lighting up of a small electric bulb, signified a telephone call, his face lost the dullness of repose and became animated and interesting. He gesticulated to the telephone as though it understood.

I remarked on the comparative stillness of his room, and he laughed. 'Wait till there is a political discussion!' he said.

Secretaries came in at intervals with letters. He opened them, signed the empty envelope, and gave it back, a form of receipt I suppose. Some papers were brought him to sign, and he signed, but whilst looking at something else instead of at his signature.

I asked him why he had women secretaries. He said because all the men were at the war, and that caused us to talk of Poland. I understood that peace with Poland had been signed yesterday, but he says not, that forces are at work trying to upset the negotiations, and that the position is very grave.

'Besides,' he said, 'when we have settled Poland, we have got Wrangel.' I asked if Wrangel was negligible, and he said that Wrangel counted quite a bit, which is a different attitude from that adopted by the other Russians I have met, who have laughed scornfully at the idea of Wrangel.

We talked about H. G. Wells, and he said that the only book of his he had read was *Joan and Peter*, but that he had not read it to the end. He liked the description at the beginning of the English intellectual bourgeois life. He admitted that he should have read, and regretted not having read, some of the earlier fantastic novels about wars in the air and the world set free. I am told that Lenin manages to get through a good deal of reading. On his desk was a volume by Chiozza Money. He asked me if I had had any trouble in getting through to his room, and I explained that Borodin had accompanied me. I then had the face to suggest that Borodin, being an extremely intelligent man who can speak good English, would make a good Ambassador to England when there is peace. Lenin looked at me with the most amused expression, his eyes seemed to see right through me, and then said: 'That would please Monsieur Churchill wouldn't it?' I asked if Winston was the most hated Englishman. He shrugged his shoulders, and then added something about Churchill being the man with all the force of the capitalists behind him. We argued about that, but he did not want to hear my opinion, his own being quite unshakeable. He talked about Winston being my cousin, and I said rather apologetically that I could not help it, and informed him that I had another cousin who was a Sinn Feiner. He laughed, and said 'That must be a cheerful party when you three get together.' I suppose it would be cheerful, but we have never all three been together!

During these four hours he never smoked, and never even drank a cup of tea. I have never worked so long on end before, and at 3.45 I could hold out no longer. I was blind with weariness and hunger, and said good-bye. He promised to sit on the revolving stand tomorrow. If all goes well, I think I ought to be able to finish him. I do hope it is good. I think it looks more like him than any of the busts I have seen yet. He has a curious Slav face, and looks very ill.

When I asked for news of England, he offered me the three latest *Daily Heralds* he had, dated September 21, 22 and 23. I brought them back and we all fell upon them, Russians and American alike. As for me, I have spent a blissful evening reading about the Irish Rebellion and the Miners' dispute, as if it were yesterday's news, and the Irene Munro and Bamberger cases. Goodness, one feels as though one had looked through a window and seen home on the horizon.

How tired I was; I had eaten nothing since 10 a.m. and dinner was not until 9 p.m. In between I ate some of my English biscuits.

OCTOBER 8TH.

Started work again in Lenin's room. I went by myself this time, and got past all the sentries with the pass that I had been given. I took my kodak with me, although I had not the necessary kodak permission. I put a coat over my arm, which hid it.

I don't know how I got through my day. I had to work on him from afar. My real chance came when a Comrade arrived for an interview, and then for the first time

Lenin sat and talked facing the window, so that I was able to see his full face and in a good light.

The Comrade remained a long time, and conversation was very animated. Never did I see anyone make so many faces. Lenin laughed and frowned, and looked thoughtful, sad, and humorous all in turn. His eyebrows twitched, sometimes they went right up, and then again they puckered together maliciously.

I watched these expressions, waited, hesitated, and then made my selection with a frantic rush – it was his screwed-up look. Wonderful! No one else has such a look, it is his alone. Every now and then he seemed to be conscious of my presence, and gave a piercing, enigmatical look in my direction. If I had been a spy pretending not to understand Russian, I wonder whether I should have learnt interesting things! The Comrade, when he left the room, stopped and looked at my work, and said the only word that I understand, which is *carascho*, it means 'good', and then said something about my having the character of the man, so I was glad.

After that Lenin consented to sit on the revolving stand. It seemed to amuse him very much. He said he never had sat so high. When I kneeled down to look at the glances from below, his face adopted an expression of surprise and embarrassment.

I laughed and asked: 'Are you unaccustomed to this attitude in woman?' At that moment a secretary came in, and I cannot think why they were both so amused. They talked rapid Russian together, and laughed a good deal.

When the secretary had gone, he became serious and asked me a few questions. Did I work hard in London? I said it was my life. How many hours a day? An average

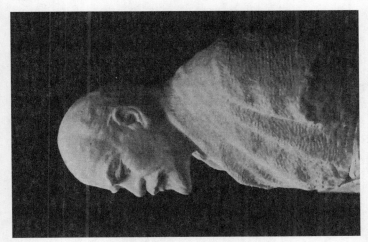

BUST OF LENIN

of seven. He made no comment on this, but it seemed to satisfy him. Until then, I had the feeling that, although he was charming to me, he looked upon me a little resentfully as a bourgeoise. I believe that he always asks people, if he does not know them, about their work and their origin, and makes up his mind about them accordingly. I showed him photographs of some of my busts and also of 'Victory'. He was emphatic in not liking the 'Victory', his point being that I had made it too beautiful.

I protested that the sacrifice involved made Victory beautiful, but he would not agree. 'That is the fault of bourgeois art, it always beautifies.'

I looked at him fiercely. 'Do you accuse me of bourgeois art?'

'I accuse you!' he answered, then held up the photograph of Dick's bust. 'I do not accuse you of embellishing this, but I pray you not to embellish me.'

He then looked at Winston. 'Is that Churchill himself? You have embellished him.' He seemed to have this on the brain.

I said: 'Give me a message to take back to Winston.'

He answered: 'I have already sent him a message through the Delegation, and he answered it not directly, but through a bitter newspaper article, in which he said I was a most horrible creature, and that our army was an army of *puces*. How you say *puces* in English? You know the French *puces*? Yes, that is it, an army of fleas. I did not mind what he said; I was glad. It showed that my message to him had angered him.'

'When will Peace come to Russia? Will a General Election bring it?' I asked.

He said: 'There is no further news of a General Election, but if Lloyd George asks for an Election it will be on anti-Bolshevism, and he may win. The Capitalists, the Court, and the military, all are behind him and Churchill.'

I asked him if he were not mistaken in his estimate of the power and popularity of Winston, and the importance and influence of the Court.

He got fiery. 'It is an intellectual bourgeois pose to say that the King does not count. He counts very much. He is the head of the Army. He is the bourgeois figurehead, and he represents a great deal, and Churchill is backed by him.' He was so insistent, so assured, so fierce about it, that I gave up the argument.

Presently, he said to me: 'What does your husband think of your coming to Russia?'

I replied that my husband was killed in the war.

'In the capitalist-imperialist war?'

I said: 'In France, 1915; what other war?'

'Ah, that is true,' he said. 'We have had so many, the imperialist, the civil war, and the war for self-defence.'

We then discussed the wonderful spirit of self-sacrifice and patriotism with which England entered upon the war in 1914, and he wanted me to read *Le Feu* and *La Clarté* of Barbusse, in which that spirit and its development is so wonderfully described.

Then the telephone gave its damnable low buzzing. He looked at his watch. He had promised me fifteen minutes on the revolving stand and given me half an hour. He got down and went to the telephone. It did not matter: I had done all I could. I had verified my measurements, and they were correct, which was a relief, and so, it being 4 o'clock and I mighty hungry, I said good-bye.

He was very pleased, said I had worked very quickly,

called in his secretary and discussed it with her, said it was *carascho*. I asked him to give orders to have it removed to my studio, Room 31. Two soldiers arrived and carried it out. I asked Lenin for his photograph, which he sent for and signed for me.

I hurried after the two panting soldiers with their load. We passed through the rooms of the astonished secretaries, out into the corridors, past the bored and surprised sentries, and got through to the main building. Two or three times they had to pause and deposit 'Lenin' on the floor, to the interest of the passers-by. At last he was safely in Room 31, and they returned to Lenin's room for the stands. It was a good long way, and they were tired and dripping with sweat when their job was done.

To my intense embarrassment, they refused money, though I offered them stacks of paper notes. They refused very amiably, but firmly. I made signs of imploration and signs of secrecy, but they laughed and just pointed to their Communist badges, and offered me their cigarettes which were precious, being rationed.

At 4 Kameneff walked in, very surprised at Lenin being finished and already back in my room. He had come in from a conference next door. He went back and fetched in the Conference; eight or more men came in, some with interesting heads, others just ordinary-looking workmen.

They all talked at once. One was Kalinin, whom I had seen in Lenin's room at an interview. Kalinin is the President of the Republic, and is a peasant elected by the peasants. He was charming and promised to sit for me, but is off to the front tonight for ten days, and offered to take me with him. He told Kameneff that as I worked so rapidly I should find some interesting heads to do there, especially General Budienny.

I said I thought it would be wonderful to do this work within sound of the guns. Kameneff promised to ring me up at 9 o'clock to tell me if I was to start at 10. Alas! It turned out to be a troop train, and not possible for a woman.

OCTOBER 9TH.

Started off in a motor with Mr. Vanderlip and some-one from the Foreign Office. We went to a textile factory, a huge place, and pronounced by Mr. Vanderlip to have the best and latest machinery, but there were 240 workers where there had been 2,500, and there were acres of machinery lying idle, the reason being lack of fuel. Mr. Vanderlip, with that unfailing American 'spread-eagle', said that 50 experienced American workers could have done the work of those 240. It is true there was a good deal of idling going on. This may have been due either to lack of sufficient work, or to the Communist system by which each man or woman is as good as another, and there is none to oversee the work. But what had been done was well done.

From there we went to one of the big fur stores which before the Revolution belonged to a private firm, but today is the property of the Government. There were rooms full of huge hampers packed with sable skins for export, and of course, as I was the only woman present, they dangled bunches of sable skins before me. Now sables don't say much to me if they are not made up, but silver foxes are different, and they cruelly put round my neck some silver foxes.

OCTOBER 10TH.

Kameneff came at midday to say good-bye to me; he is off to the front tomorrow for an indefinite time. He brought with him a young man with close-cropped hair and clear-cut features, calling himself Alexandre. Kameneff thinks Alexandre may be able to take care of me during his absence. I certainly need someone, as Michael Borodin goes to Madrid on Tuesday, and then I do not know what will become of me. Kameneff discussed with me about the government buying the Russian copyright of my heads. He then asked me to make a list of things I wanted, and that he could do for me before he goes. I had several wants: for one thing, I am extremely cold. The coat I arrived in is only cloth – now there is snow on the ground, and the river begins to freeze. I have to wrap my rug round my shoulders when I go out. The peasants are far better off, they have all appeared in sheepskin coats, the fur they wear inside, and the leather, which is usually stained deep orange or rust colour, is a very decorative exterior. The bourgeois women have brought out their former remains of splendour, and although they may have only felt or canvas shoes on their feet, and a shawl over their heads, some of them wear coats that one would turn round to look at in Bond Street. I headed my list of requirements with the request for a coat – as well as caviare, Trotsky, and a soldier of the Red Army whom I want to model. Trotsky is expected back from the front in a few days. It is a bore that Kameneff is going away, but Alexandre promised to arrange sittings for me.

OCTOBER 11TH.

In the morning I accompanied Michael Borodin to the

headquarters of the Third International. It is a beautiful house, formerly the German Embassy, and where Mirbach was murdered.

I came away in a car with Madame Balabanoff, of whom I had often heard. She is small, past middle age, with a crumpled-up face, but intelligent. I did not find her any too amiable on our way to the Kremlin, where she dropped me.

She told me that it was absurd that any bust of Lenin or anyone else should be done, the theory being that the cause, not the individuals, should count. The humblest person who suffers privation for the cause is equally as important as any of the legislators, she explained, and proceeded to assure me that no picture or bust of herself existed, nor ever should. Happily I had not asked her to sit for me. She practically told me that I was doing Lenin's head to take back to England to show to the idle curious. I corrected her by saying that, so far as the public was concerned, I only wished to enable those who had him at present represented by a photograph, to substitute a bust. She was equally vehement about the photograph. Perhaps she expects to alter human nature.

Before I got out of the car, she assured me that her tirade was in no way personal and would I, please, not misunderstand her.

OCTOBER 14TH.

Michael Borodin found me after breakfast, miserably wrapped in my rug, shivering with cold and depression, and with tears irrepressibly streaming down my face. I had several grievances which had been accumulating for some days, and at last my patience had come to a head. The fact is I had heard of a courier having arrived yesterday from London, and no one had taken the trouble to find out if there were any letters for me. Ever since I left England on September 11th I have not had one word of news, nor answers to two telegrams that Kameneff sent for me asking after the children. Secondly, I had not been given the coat that Kameneff had ordered for me, so it was impossible to go out as it was too cold.

Michael for the first time seemed really moved. He wrapped me round in his fur coat, went off to the garden and fetched up a load of wood for me (I had never known him do such a thing before), and lit my fire himself. Then he telephoned to the Foreign Office. There were no letters for me, but some bundles for Kameneff. He also got hold of Comrade Alexandre on the telephone to know when I was going to have the promised coat, and altogether was very helpful. His journey to Madrid has been delayed daily, but he is to start tomorrow. It seems to me that in Russia one only knows about ten minutes beforehand what one is going to do! They are divinely vague.

OCTOBER 15TH.

I went to the Kremlin to meet Comrade Alexandre there at midday: he was to bring me a soldier as a model. Not feeling brave enough to go and review a platoon and make my own selection, I had described exactly what I wanted: not the bloodthirsty savage Bolshevik of English tradition, but the dreamy-eyed young Slav who knows what he is fighting for, and such as I passed every day on the parade ground. I waited in my studio impatiently till 2 o'clock, and then Alexandre arrived accompanied by a soldier who was typically neither

Russian, nor military, nor intellectual, nor even fine physically. He was small, white, *chêtif*, and had a waxed moustache. It was a bad moment. I tried to hide my disappointment and my amusement. I missed lunching in order to work on him, and began something that was not in the least like my model, but was the product of my imagination. At 5 I came home tired and hungry and cold. I lay down on my sofa and watched the dusk crawl up behind the Kremlin. At 8.30 I was called down to the telephone, which is in the kitchen. It was Borodin speaking from the Foreign Office. He said 'good-bye' in his abrupt manner. 'This is the right way,' he said. 'This is the way it should be.' The maid was throwing her broom around the kitchen, making as much noise as possible, and a strange man glared at me out of the gloom. I found it difficult to concentrate my attention. Michael knows that I do not believe in 'futures', but nevertheless we said 'someday', and I wonder very much if that strange Communist-Revolutionary, with his mask-like face and deep voice, will ever cross my path again. Tonight I regret him, but then I am lonely for the moment – friendless, and this is a place where one needs friends.

At 9 o'clock, not having eaten since 10 a.m., I went downstairs to round-up some food. There, to my surprise, I met Litvinoff, who had been in Moscow since the day before yesterday. Our pleasure at seeing each other again was mutual and spontaneous. He is coming to stay at our house, and will occupy the vacated room of Borodin.

OCTOBER 16TH.

Comrade Alexandre came to see me at 9 p.m., to tell me that he could not arrange with Trotsky for sittings.

I gathered that Trotsky had been emphatic and brusque in his refusal, but after all, I have done Lenin, and he is the one who counts most. I can go back to England without the head of Trotsky, but I could not have gone without the head of Lenin. I *have* accomplished what I came for, and so to hell with Trotsky!

Alexandre said he could only stay ten minutes, but he left at midnight. He talked Communism the whole time. Now Borodin unfurled his Communist spirit to me slowly, because he knew me, and to what I belonged, and he realised that the thing hurled at me in a crude mass would stagger me. He led me up to it with great caution. Alexandre, on the other hand, with no understanding or sympathy, took all my inborn prejudices and just broke them, stamped on them, metaphorically spat on them, and gave me a big feed of unadulterated Communism. He is a fanatic, and left me breathless and wondering. All was well until we got to the children part: he said that his wife had to work, so their baby, who is six weeks old, has to go by day to the Crèche.

'Are you satisfied with the care it gets at the Crèche?' I asked him. He shrugged his shoulders, said that collectively they could not receive the same attention as they would if they were cared for individually. He then volunteered the information that of course the baby was more liable to get ill and even die if it was in the Crèche, but that it was a chance, and after all his wife's life was not going to be reduced to feeding, washing, and dressing a baby. That was no sort of existence, and so, what alternative was there except the Crèche?

It was the cold, dispassionate way in which he said it that gave me the creeps.

'What is your wife's work?' I said.

'Politics, same as mine,' he said.

'Are you fond of your baby?'

'Yes.'

'Is your wife fond of it?'

'Yes.'

I thought to myself that she has not had to pray for a baby, and weep because the months went by. She has not had to wait, and wait – it is not infinitely precious to her, her baby.

He then counter-questioned me:

'What did you do with your children when you became a widow and had no home?'

'My parents took them.'

'And if you had had no parents who could take them? How could you have worked?'

It is true that there must be thousands of women who earn their living and have no family in the background on whom to plant the baby. What happens in a country where there is no paternal State? In Russia the State will clothe, feed and educate them from birth until fourteen years of age. They may go to the Crèche for the day or permanently. Children may go to the State school for the half day, whole day, or to board. Their parents may see them, or give them up for ever, as they choose, and there is no difference made between the legitimate and the illegitimate child. Moreover, according to the labour laws, no woman may work for eight weeks before the baby is born, nor for eight weeks after birth. She is sent away to a rest-house in the country, always of course at the State's expense. On application she is given the necessary layette for the new born. It is difficult to preserve one's maternal sentimentality in the face of this Communistic generosity.

OCTOBER 17TH.

I stayed in bed all day as I felt ill, and there was nothing better to do. Litvinoff came in to see me in the afternoon and was surprised that I had not begun to work on Trotsky. I explained to him that, through Comrade Alexandre, Trotsky had flatly refused to let me do him. Litvinoff could not understand this, but said he had seen Trotsky last night. It was then decided that Litvinoff would see Trotsky again during the day, and telephone to me what arrangements he could make. He then left me, to come back again in a few minutes bringing something preciously in both hands. It was a hen's egg. As I have not seen one since I have been in Moscow I stifled my instinctive aversion to accepting valuable presents from men and had the egg fried for dinner.

OCTOBER 18TH.

Trotsky's car came for me punctually at 11.30 a.m. (usually the cars that are ordered are an hour late, and people keep their appointments two hours late. Trotsky and Lenin are, I hear, the only two exceptions to the rule). I made Litvinoff come and tell the chauffeur that he was first to go to the Kremlin with me to fetch my things. When we got to the big round building in the Kremlin in which I have my studio, I took the chauffeur to the pass office and explained by signs by showing my own pass that I required one for the chauffeur. This was done. It is satisfactory to have arrived at the stage when I get the pass for someone else, instead of someone else getting it for me. Kameneff told me the other day that I walk into the Kremlin with the air of one who belonged to it.

Trotsky's chauffeur, myself, and the plaster moulder who was there, working, carried the things down to the car, and I was driven to a place some way off, the War Ministry, I think. Getting in was not easy, as I had no pass, and there was an altercation with the sentry. I understood the chauffeur explaining: 'Yes, yes, it's the English sculptor', but the sentry was adamant. He shrugged his shoulders, said he didn't care, and made a blank face. I had to wait until a secretary came to fetch me. He took me upstairs, through two rooms of soldier-secretaries. In the end room there was a door guarded by a sentry, and next to that door a big writing table from which someone telephoned through into the next room to know if I could come in. Unlike Lenin's, not even his secretaries go in to see Trotsky without telephoning first for permission. It was not without some trepidation, having heard how very intractable he is, and knowing his sister,[1] that I was ushered in – I and my modelling stand and my clay together.

I had instantly the pleasurable sensation of a room that is sympathetic, big, well-proportioned and simple.

From behind an enormous writing table in one corner near the window came forth Trotsky. He shook hands with me welcomingly, though without a smile, and asked if I talked French.

He offered courteously to assist me in moving my stand into the right place, and even to have his mammoth table moved into some other position if the light was not right.

The light from the two windows was certainly very bad, but although he said: 'Move anything and do just

1   Madame Leo Kameneff.

whatever you like', there was nothing one could do that would help. The room, which would have made a beautiful ballroom, loomed large and dark. There were huge white columns which got in my way and hampered the light. My heart sank at the difficulties of the situation. I looked at my man, who was bending down, writing at his desk. Impossible to see his face. I looked at him and then at my clay, in despair. Then I went and knelt in front of the writing table opposite him, with my chin on his papers. He looked up from his writing and stared back, a perfectly steady, unabashed stare. His look was a solemn, analytical one, perhaps mine was too. After a few seconds, realising the absurdity of our attitudes, I had to laugh, and said: 'I hope you don't mind being looked at.' 'I don't mind,' he said. 'I have my *revanche* in looking at you, and it is I who gain.'

He then ordered a fire to be lit because he thought it was cold for me. It was not cold, it was overheated, but the sound and sight of the fire were nice. A matronly peasant-woman with a handkerchief tied round her head came and lit it. He said he liked her because she walked softly, and had a musical voice. Curious that he should admire in another what is so characteristic of himself; his voice is unusually melodious.

Seeing that he was prepared to be amiable, I asked him if I could bother him with measurements. *'Tout ce que vous voudrez,'* he said, and pointed out to me how unsymmetrical his face is. He opened his mouth and snapped his teeth to show me that his underjaw is crooked, and as he did so he reminded me of a snarling wolf. When he talks his face lights up and his eyes flash. Trotsky's eyes are much talked of in Russia, and he is called 'the wolf'. His nose also is crooked and looks as though it had been broken. If it were straight he would have a very fine line from the forehead. Full-face he is Mephisto. His eyebrows go up at an angle, and the lower part of his face tapers into a pointed and defiant beard. As I measured him with calipers, he remarked: *'Vous me caressez avec des instruments d'acier.'* He talks very rapid, and very fluent French, and could easily be mistaken for a Frenchman. I dragged my modelling stand across the room to try for a better light on the other side. He watched me with a weary look, and said: 'Even in clay you make me travel, and I am so tired of travelling.' He explained to me that he is not as desperately busy as usual because there is Peace with Poland, and good news from the South. I told him that I had nearly gone to the Southern front with Kalinin, who wanted to take me, but that Kameneff wouldn't let me go because it was a troop train. Without hesitating a moment he answered:

'Do you want to go to the front? You can come with me.'

He was thoughtful for a while, and then asked me: 'Are you under the care here of our Foreign Office?'

I said I was not.

'But who are you here with? Who is responsible for you?'

'Kameneff,' I said.

'But Kameneff is at the front.'

'Yes.'

'Then you are alone? H'm, that is very dangerous in a revolutionary country. Do you know Karahan, Tchicherin's secretary?'

'Yes; he is living in our house, so is Litvinoff.'

'Ah, Litvinoff, I will ring him up.'

He did ring him up, but what he said I could not

understand. Litvinoff told me later that Trotsky had asked him if I was all right, and if it would be indiscreet or not to show me the front. Litvinoff gave me a good character.

At 4 o'clock he ordered tea, and had some with me. He talked to me about himself, and of his wanderings in exile during the war, and how, finally, at the outbreak of the Revolution, he sailed on a neutral ship from the United States to return to Russia; how the British arrested him and took him to a Canadian concentration camp. He was detained a few months, until the Russian Government succeeded in obtaining his release.

He was particularly incensed at the British interfering with the movements of a man who was not going to Britain, nor from a British colony, nor by a British ship: 'But I had a good time in that camp,' he said. 'There were a lot of German sailors there, and I did some propaganda work. By the time I left they were all good revolutionaries, and I still get letters from some of them.'

At 5 I prepared to leave. He said that I looked tired. I said I was tired from battling with my work in such a bad light. He suggested trying by electric light, and we agreed on 7 o'clock the next evening. He sent me home in his car.

OCTOBER 19TH.

Trotsky's car came at 6.30. Nicholas Andrev had been having tea with me, and I offered to give him a lift, as he lives somewhere near the War Ministry. It was snowing hard and there was a driving wind, which lifted up the frozen snow and blew it about like white smoke. The car had a hood, but no sides. In the Red Square we punctured. For some time we sat patiently watching the passers-by falling down on the slippery pavement, and the horse-carts struggling up the hill. Winter has come very suddenly and one month too soon. The horses have not yet been shod for the slippery roads, consequently they can hardly stand up. This morning I counted four down all at the same moment. In London a fallen horse attracts a good deal of attention, and a crowd collects, but here no one even turns his head to look. I have been much laughed at because I stop to watch, but the method of getting the horse up amuses me. The driver (man or woman, as the case may be) gets behind and pushes the cart. The horse, so weak that he has no resisting power, impelled forward by the shafts, struggles to his feet in spite of himself. No unharnessing is necessary. This evening, when I became too cold to be interested any longer by the passers-by falling in the square, I asked the chauffeur if he had nearly finished. He answered 'Sichas' which literally translated is 'immediately', but in practice means tomorrow, or next week! So I pulled up the fur collar of my inadequate cloth coat, put my feet up lengthways on the seat, and let Andrev sit on them to keep them warm. I arrived at Trotsky's at 7.30. He looked at me and then at the clock. I explained what had happened. 'So that is the reason of your inexactitude,' he said; an inexactitude which could not in the least inconvenience him as he did not have to wait for me. He kissed my frozen hand, and put two chairs for me by the fire, one for me and one for my feet. When I had melted and turned on all the lights of the crystal candelabra he said: 'We will have an agreement, quite businesslike; I shall come and stand by the side of your work for five minutes every half hour.' Of course the five minutes got very enlarged, and we talked and worked and lost all track of time. When the telephone rang he asked: 'Have I your permission?' His manners are charming. I said to him: 'I cannot get over it, how amiable and courteous you are. I understood you were a very disagreeable man. What am I to say to people in England when they ask me: "What sort of a monster is Trotsky?"' With a mischievous look he said: 'Tell them in England, tell them—' (but I cannot tell them!). I said to him: 'You are not a bit like your sister.' The shadow of a smile crossed his face, but he did not answer.

I showed him photographs of my work and he kept the ones of the 'Victory'. Among the portraits he liked 'Asquith' best, and said that that one was worked with more feeling and care than any of the others. He took for granted that Asquith must like me, which is not necessarily the case, and said half-laughingly: 'You have given me an idea – if Asquith comes back into office *soon* (there is a rumour that he might bring in a Coalition with Labour, and recognise Russia) I will hold you as a hostage until England makes peace with us.' I laughed: 'What you are saying humorously is what a British official told me seriously, only he said it à propos of Winston. As a matter of fact, I'd be proud if I could be of any use in the cause of peace. But if you said you would shoot me, Winston would only say "shoot"' – which is, to my mind, the right spirit, and exactly the spirit that prevails among the Bolsheviks. They would not hesitate to shoot me (some of them have told me so) if it were necessary, even if they liked me as a woman. Winston is the only man I know in England who is made of the stuff that Bolsheviks are made of. He has fight, force and fanaticism.

Towards the end of the evening, as Trotsky said

nothing more about the project of my going to the front, I asked him if he had decided to take me or not. He said: 'It is for you to decide if you wish to come – but I shall not start for three or four days.' It was getting late and he looked very tired. He was standing in front of the clay with his back to it, so that I had the two profiles exactly in line. His eyes were shut and he swayed. For a moment I feared he was going to faint. One does not think of Trotsky as a man who faints, but anything may happen to a man who works as he does. My thought was of my work, and I said to him: 'Do not fall backward, or you fall on my work.' He answered quickly: '*Je tombe toujours en avant!*' I asked him to order the motor, having realised that unless he sends for it I have to wait outside in the cold or look for it in the garage. While the car was coming round he sent for a reproduction of a portrait of himself by an artist friend of his, to show me that the same difficulties that I am having with his jaw and chin were experienced also by the draughtsman who only succeeded in this, the last of a great many sketches. It is evidently one that Trotsky likes, for it is reproduced in colour in almost every office one goes into. I told him I wanted it and he wrote upon it 'Tovarisch (which means Comrade) Clare Sheridan', and signed it. This has its effect on the Bolsheviks who have been into my room and seen it.

OCTOBER 20TH.

Comrade Alexandre telephoned that he would fetch me at 1 o'clock to go to the fur store. I suppose the intense cold had at last moved either his pity or his anxiety for me. Before I left Vanderlip said that if there were any choice, and I was fool enough not to choose a sable coat, he would never speak to me again. The threat left me unmoved. It is only on occasions of necessity, when we exchange valuable presents (say a new tooth brush for a box of pills), that we have an armistice. On the way to the fur store Alexandre picked up another man, unknown but very nice, with whom I talked a mixture of English and German. We went to one of the biggest storehouses in Moscow, which, like all the rest, had been a private firm, but has been requisitioned by the Government. It was a cave-like building, dark and stone cold. We went up in a cage lift to what seemed to be the attic. It was low and long and dark, and an arc-light barely lit up the corner. Coats hung from the ceiling like so many hundred Bluebeard wives.

I took off mine to try on. An old man who looked like Moses and spoke German showed me the best and told me to make my choice. Alexandre looked on with a grim smile, and asked if I were the proverbial woman, or whether I would make my choice within reasonable limits of time. It was not easy. The coats dated back three years, and some were even too old-fashioned for Moscow. I liked a brown Siberian pony lined with ermine, but the moth had got into the pony. I liked a broadtail, but it was thin as cloth; they offered to have it fur-lined for me, but my need was immediate. There was a mink, but it had an old-fashioned flounce. There were astrachans, but everyone in Moscow has astrachan, it seemed too ordinary. I felt bewildered. My attention then wandered to a row of shubas: big sleeveless cloaks of velvet, that wrap around one, and descend to one's feet. There was a dream lined with blue fox, and another with white. My friends put one round my shoulders, it was lined with sable: light as a feather, and warm as a nest. I despairingly voiced the fact that I could not walk about the streets of Moscow in a wine coloured velvet and sable cape. They said I could, but then they were wrong. 'I look much too bourgeoise, I shall be shot!'

'You won't be shot, and sable is good enough for a good worker.' I showed a sable stole to Alexandre and told him it was the blackest and most beautiful bit of sable one could find. He shrugged his shoulders with perfect indifference, and said he knew nothing about it. Finally I walked out in a very practical black Siberian pony lined with grey squirrel, divinely warm, though rather heavy, and Alexandre said to me: 'Now you can say that you have shared in the Government distribution of bourgeois property to the people.'

At 7.30 p.m. Trotsky sent his car for me, but a soldier stopped us before we even reached the block where the War Ministry is. The whole bit of road was being especially guarded. The reason for this is that foreign papers have announced an impending counter-Revolution, but if there is any such plot their warning has been given most obligingly in time, and steps have been taken to deal with it. The town is placarded with notices that inhabitants must not be out after midnight. It gave one just a small thrill, and there have been none so far. This evening when I arrived Trotsky stood by the fire while I was warming, and I asked him for news. He says that the German workers have voted in favour of joining the Moscow International which is very important. 'England is our only real and dangerous enemy,' he said. 'Not France?' I asked. 'No, France is just a noisy, hysterical woman, making scenes: but England – that is different altogether.' He talked about the persistence of the foreign Press in decrying the stability of the Soviet

Government. All the governments of Europe, he said, had undergone changes in the last three years; he pointed to France, Italy, the Central Powers, Turkey, and finally Poland. The British Government was holding out longer than any other, but that was pretty rocky, and its ministers were constantly changing their posts. The Soviet Government was the oldest government in Europe, and the only one in which the ministers retained their posts and displayed any unity, and this in spite of every effort on the part of the world to dislodge them.

He then busied himself at his table with papers. I worked for an hour and we never spoke, but he never disregarded me as Lenin did. I could walk round Lenin and look at him from all sides, he remained absorbed in his reading, and apparently oblivious of my presence. Whenever I go near Trotsky he looks up from his work sharply with piercing eyes and I forget which part of his face I was intent upon. Towards the end of the evening, when even my tiptoe stalking had aroused him, he asked me: '*Avez vous besoin de moi.*' I replied yes, as always. He came and stood by the clay, but he is very critical, and watches it and me all the time, and makes me nervous. I undid and did over again a good deal. The room was hot, and the clay got dry, it was uphill work. Never have I done anyone so difficult. He is subtle and irregular. At one moment the bust looked like Scipio Africanus, and I could see he was dissatisfied; then when I had altered it and asked him what he thought he stood for some time in silence with a suppressed smile before he let himself go: 'It looks like a French *bon bourgeois*, who admires the woman who is doing him, but he has no connection with Communism.'

Happily the peasant woman came in with tea, and I

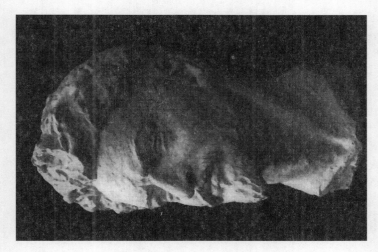

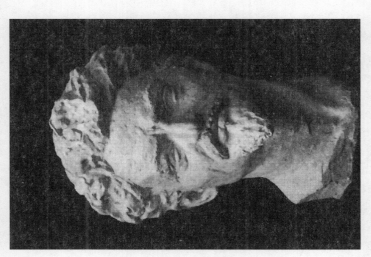

BUST OF TROTSKY

sat down wearily with my head in my hands, utterly dispirited and discouraged. Only the fierce determination to make it come right roused me and I went at it again. He said, as he watched me: 'When your teeth are clenched and you are fighting with your work, *vous êtes encore femme.*' I asked him to take off his pince-nez, as they hampered me. He hates doing this, he says he feels *désarmé* and absolutely lost without them. It seemed akin to physical pain taking them off – they have become part of him and the loss of them completely changes his individuality. It is a pity, as they rather spoil an otherwise classical head.

While he was standing there helplessly with half-closed eyes, he remarked on my name being spelt in the same way as that of the playwright. I explained that I had married a direct descendant. He was interested and said *The School for Scandal* and *The Rivals* had been translated and were occasionally acted here in Russian. He then got on to Shakespeare. I wish I could recall the words in which he described his appreciation, exclaiming finally: 'If England had never produced anything else, she would have justified her existence.' We disagreed as to Byron and Shelley. He, like others I have met here, preferred Byron, and insisted in spite of my assertions to the contrary that Byron was the greater Revolutionary of the two. He was surprised that I loved Swinburne. He said he would have thought me too much of this world to love the spirituality of Swinburne. I said: 'One has one's dreams.' He gave a sigh. 'Yes,' he said, 'we all have our dreams—'

When, at the end of the evening, I was dissatisfied with my work and feeling suicidal I asked him:

'May I come back and work tomorrow night?'

'And the night after,' he answered, and added, laughing, that he would rig the place up as a studio for me, and that I could do General Kameneff after I'd finished him. General Kameneff (who is no relation to Leo Kameneff) is the Commander-in-Chief, and was a very distinguished Tsarist officer. I hear that he strongly warned the War Ministry against advancing too far towards Warsaw, and foretold the débâcle that has since been fulfilled. But he was not listened to, perhaps because of his Tsarist tradition. Probably his opinion is more respected now. Trotsky asked me if I would like to do Tchicherin, and I explained that never before had I worked under such difficult conditions, and that although I had made efforts for Lenin and himself I did not feel like doing it again for anyone else. He was quite indignant and said: 'What difficulty have you had in working here?' True it was a perfectly good room and excellent light, but Tchicherin would not move out of his Commissariat and that would mean new conditions to adapt oneself to, nor does anyone understand the difficulties of moving the finished work back to the Kremlin. Trotsky swept my excuses aside: 'Of course you must do Tchicherin – it is almost a diplomatic obligation on his part to be done.'

It was a quarter to midnight when I prepared to stop work and looked desperately at the clock: 'What about this order – how am I to be home at midnight?' I asked. He said, 'I will take you myself.' At about half after midnight we left. A man in uniform joined us and sat next to the driver. He had in his hands a very big leather holster. We started off by going in the opposite direction to the right one, and I had to try and describe the way to them. We turned back, and crossing the bridge we were stopped by five soldiers. The man with the holster had to show our papers by the light of the car lamp. It delayed us several minutes. I said to Trotsky: 'Put your head out of the window and say who you are.' *'Taisez-vous,'* said Trotsky peremptorily. I sat rebuked and silent until we were able to pass on unrecognised. He explained afterwards that he did not want them to hear a woman's voice in the car talking English. I was talking French as we always do together, and did not see that it mattered to anyone in this country whether there is a woman in a Government car or not – but I did not argue.

OCTOBER 21ST.

I did very little during the day, so as to be fresh for my night's work, though I went to see my friend the plaster-moulder who is working for so many thousand roubles a day in my studio. He is making piece moulds of the busts, so that I can leave duplicates when I go. I asked Andrev why he had to be paid so much. Andrev explained that he is the only moulder in Moscow, so he can ask what he likes: 'He says he will work for this and not for that', and Andrev held a thousand rouble note in one hand and a hundred rouble note in the other. 'But it is all the same really, only it is a different pattern', and he laughed. Certainly money has no value here, and no meaning. At 8 o'clock I went back again to the War Commissariat in Trotsky's car. On arrival I told him that I had got to get this work right tonight, and that he was not to be critical and look at it all the time and make me nervous.

He was surprised; said that he had no idea that he had that effect on me, that all he wanted was to help: *'Je veux travailler cela avec vous.'* His criticism, he said, was caused by intense interest, and that for nothing in the world would he be discouraging. He promised, however, to be good, and offer no opinion until asked. It was a better night for work; I felt calmer and it went pretty well.

The worst difficulties were surmounted. Trotsky stood for me in a good light and dictated to his stenographer. That was excellent. His face was animated and his attention occupied. I got all one side of his face done. Then came the question of the other side. He laughed, suggested another dictation, offered to stand in another position, and called back his stenographer. When we were alone again he came and stood close beside the clay and we talked while I went on working. We talked a little about myself.

He said I should remain in Russia a while longer, and do some big work, something like my 'Victory'. An emaciated and exhausted figure, but still fighting; that is the allegory of the Soviet.

I answered him that I could get no news of my children, and therefore must go back.

'I must return to my own world, to my own conventional people whose first thought is always for what the world will think. Russia with its absence of hypocrisy and pose, Russia with its big ideas, has spoilt me for my own world.'

'Ah! that is what you say now, but when you are away—' and he hesitated.

Then suddenly turning on me, with clenched teeth and fire in his eyes, he shook a threatening finger in my face: 'If, when you get back to England, *vous nous calomniez* as the rest have, I tell you that I will come to England *et je vous*—' He did not say what he would do, but there was murder in his face.

I smiled: 'That is all right. Now I know how to get you to England.' Then (to fall in with his mood): 'How can I go back and abuse the hospitality and the chivalrous treatment I have received?'

He said: 'It is not abusing, but there are ways of criticising even without abuse. It is easy enough here to be blinded *par les saletés et les souffrances* and to see no further than that, and people are apt to forget that there is no birth without suffering and horror, and Russia is in the throes of a great *accouchement*.'

He talks well, he is full of imagery and his voice is beautiful.

We paused for tea, and I talked to him of things I had heard about the schools. In reply he said he had heard no adverse reports of the co-education scheme for boys and girls. There might be an individual case of failure, though even of such a case he had not heard. He then compared the present system with that of boy colleges of his own day, and he said that his own boy of fourteen had nicer ideas about girls, and far less cynicism, than he had at the same age. The boy apparently confides in his mother, so he knows something about it.

Tonight he sent me home alone in his car; he excused himself, saying it was the only time it was possible for him to walk. He kissed my dirty hand and said that he would always preserve a memory of '*une femme avec auréole de cheveux et des mains très sales*'.

OCTOBER 22ND.

Finished!

I worked until half after midnight. I think it is a success. He said so; but it has been such a struggle.

About half way through the evening, the electric lights

went out. A secretary lit four candles. On the telephone Trotsky learnt that the lights had gone out all over the town.

I asked him hopefully if it could possibly be the outburst of a counter-Revolution.

He laughed and asked if that was what I wanted.

I said that I thought it would break the monotony.

Until the lights went on I read the leading article on Bolshevism in *The Times* of, I think, October 4th. He had several English papers on his desk and we read together with much amusement that he (Trotsky) had been wounded, and that General Budienny had been court-martialled. There were even descriptions of barricades in the streets of Moscow: someone must have mistaken the stacks of fuel that the tramcars are bringing in and unloading every day. When the lights went on I worked hectically until half after midnight, with the desperation of knowing it was the last sitting.

At midnight he was standing by the side of the work, rather tired and very still and patient, when suddenly I had the thought of asking him to undo his collar for me. He unbuttoned his tunic and the shirt underneath, and laid bare a splendid neck and chest. I worked like a fury for half an hour which was all too short. I tried to convey into my clay some of his energy and vitality. I worked with the desperation that always accompanies last moments. When I left he said to me: '*Eh bien! on ira ensemble au front?*' But something tells me that we shall never meet again. I feel that it is almost worth while to preserve the impression of our hours of individual work, collaboration and quietude, silently guarded by a sentry with fixed bayonet outside the door. To let in the light of day would be to spoil it.

There is a French saying: '*On n'est pas toujours né dans son pays.*' It equally follows that all are not born in their rightful sphere. Trotsky is one of these. At one time, in his youth, what was he? A Russian exile in a journalist's office. Even then I am told he was witty, but with the wit of bitterness. Now he has come into his own and has unconsciously developed a new individuality. He has the manner and ease of a man born to a great position; he has become a statesman, a ruler, a leader. But if Trotsky were not Trotsky, and the world had never heard of him, one would still appreciate his very brilliant mind. The reason I have found him so much more difficult to do than I expected is on account of his triple personality. He is the cultured, well-read man, he is the vituperative fiery politician, and he can be the mischievous laughing school-boy with a dimple in his cheek. All these three I have seen in turn, and have had to converge them into clay interpretation.

OCTOBER 23RD.

I went in the morning to fetch away the bust and take it to my room in the Kremlin. I went at 11, before Trotsky had got there. His motor was at my disposal and three men to convey the precious work away. These are the moments that take years off my life! It arrived, however, undamaged, which was little short of a triumph. When my plaster-moulder saw it he exclaimed with pleasure. Apparently it is very like, and everyone is pleased. As Trotsky is adored, I take it as a great compliment to my work that it is considered good enough.

The relief of having accomplished him as well as Lenin is indescribable. I wake up in the night and wonder if it is true or a dream. Now I am completely happy. I have achieved my purpose. I have proved myself to these people, and they in return have proved their belief in me by their trouble and courteousness. I am no longer harassed by anxieties and fears. Those who discouraged me in the early days treat me now with respect, consideration and even admiration. I am happy, I am happy! I sing when I wake in the morning, I sing when I wash in cold water, I come down to my breakfast of black bread with a lighter step!

I breakfast every morning with Litvinoff. By coming down at 11 the others have finished, so we can talk. If Rothstein is present the conversation becomes Russian. If Vanderlip is there he talks all the time about America (he usually leaves the room with boredom if conversation is on any other subject). It is the fashion in Europe to vilify Litvinoff and to regard him as a terribly dangerous man. I suppose that he is an astute diplomatist. Whatever he is, he is better than he pretends, and though he gets no credit for it, he has done a good deal for the British prisoners here. He has unfortunately an abrupt manner, and a way of refusing to do things by pretending that they are no concern of his, but straightaway he will go off and do a kindness to the very people who are damning him for having refused. To me he is charming, frank, outspoken, and always ready to help.

OCTOBER 24TH.

We have all been very much saddened by the death from typhus of John Reed, the American Communist. Everyone liked him and his wife, Louise Bryant, the War Correspondent. She is quite young and had only recently joined him. He had been here two years, and Mrs. Reed, unable to obtain a passport, finally came in through

Murmansk. Everything possible was done for him, but of course there are no medicaments here: the hospitals are cruelly short of necessities. He should not have died, but he was one of those young, strong men, impatient of illness, and in the early stages he would not take care of himself.

I attended his funeral. It is the first funeral without a religious service that I have ever seen. It did not seem to strike anyone else as peculiar, but it was to me. His coffin stood for some days in the Trades' Union Hall, the walls of which are covered with huge revolutionary cartoons in marvellously bright decorative colouring. We all assembled in that hall. The coffin stood on a dais and was covered with flowers. As a bit of staging it was very effective, but I saw, when they were being carried out, that most of the wreaths were made of tin flowers painted. I suppose they do service for each Revolutionary burial.

There was a great crowd, but people talked very low. I noticed a Christ-like man with long, fair curly hair, and a fair beard and clear blue eyes; he was quite young. I asked who he was. No one seemed to know. 'An artist of sorts,' someone suggested. Not all the people with wonderful heads are wonderful people. Mr. Rothstein and I followed the procession to the grave, accompanied by a band playing a Funeral March that I had never heard before. Whenever that Funeral March struck up (and it had a tedious refrain), everyone uncovered; it seemed to be the only thing they uncovered for. We passed across the Place de la Révolution, and through the sacred gate to the Red Square. He was buried under the Kremlin wall next to all the Revolutionaries his Comrades. As a background to his grave was a large Red banner nailed upon the wall with the letters in gold: 'The leaders die, but the cause lives on.'

When I was first told that this was the burying ground of the Revolutionaries I looked in vain for graves, and I saw only a quarter of a mile or so of green grassy bank. There was not a memorial, a headstone or a sign, not even an individual mound. The Communist ideal seemed to have been realised at last: the Equality, unattainable in life, the Equality for which Christ died, had been realisable only in death.

A large crowd assembled for John Reed's burial and the occasion was one for speeches. Bucharin and Madame Kolontai both spoke. There were speeches in English, French, German and Russian. It took a very long time, and a mixture of rain and snow was falling. Although the poor widow fainted, her friends did not take her away. It was extremely painful to see this white-faced, unconscious woman lying back on the supporting arm of a Foreign Office official, more interested in the speeches than in the human agony.

The faces of the crowd around betrayed neither sympathy nor interest, they looked on unmoved. I could not get to her, as I was outside the ring of soldiers who stood guard nearly shoulder to shoulder. I marvel continuously at the blank faces of the Russian people. In France or Italy one knows that in moments of sorrow the people are deeply moved, their arms go round one, and their sympathy is overwhelming. They cry with our sorrows, they laugh with our joys. But Russia seems numb. I wonder if it has always been so or whether the people have lived through years of such horror that they have become insensible to pain.

Happily no salute was fired. The last time the machine guns rattled at a burial I heard them in my studio, which is just the other side of the wall. On that occasion the old porter who takes care of me at the Kremlin told me that his wife nearly died of heart failure – she thought the 'Whites' had come. Probably it affects other jumpy people in the same way.

Here the terror of the Whites is as great as is, on the other side, the terror of the Reds! The poor people do not want any more fighting. I think they are quite indifferent as to who rules them, they want only Peace.

When I got back I found Maxim Litvinoff, who also had been at the funeral and had looked for me in the crowd in vain. He says that he has arranged with Tchicherin that I am to begin him tomorrow. I have not asked to do him, but if it is all arranged for me I am only too delighted. But I do not look forward to working at the Commissariat for Foreign Affairs. It is the Hotel Metropole, in the Place de la Révolution, and although it will not be necessary to have a pass, and there will be none of the sentry difficulties as with Lenin and Trotsky, the drain-smells are such that one climbs the stairs two at a time holding one's breath! There are bits of the Kremlin that are enough to kill the healthiest person, but the Metropole baffles all description. Inside the offices it is all right, but the double windows everywhere are hermetically sealed for the winter, and I wonder that people do not die like flies. Litvinoff tells me that a new building is almost ready and that the next time I come to Moscow there will be a beautiful Commissariat. It is curious that in Moscow, which was one of the richest cities in the world and contained more rich merchants than almost any other, something more was not done for sanitation. Last year owing to lack of fuel most of the pipes in the town burst. No wonder there was an epidemic of typhus. This year things are better organised, and if there is Peace on the two fronts, conditions may be enormously improved.

This evening Comrade Alexandre took me to a play. He gave me my choice, and I decided that *La Fille de Madame Angot*, being an operetta, would be more amusing that *Twelfth Night* in Russian. It was at the Théâtre des Arts, where Tchekov's plays used to be produced. Tchekov is no longer acted; he wrote for a class that is temporarily extinct; the workers and peasants would not understand it. Afterwards, coming home in the motor, I noticed a tremendous glare in the sky, it obviously meant a fire, and I insisted on going to look for it. If the fire, when found, was disappointing, at least the search for it was interesting, and revealed to me the unsuspected size of Moscow. We drove through miles of deserted streets, where we met only a few soldiers wearily trudging through the mud. We shouted to them: 'Tovarischi, where is the fire?' There is something very pleasant in hailing a complete stranger as a Comrade – one feels at once a link of friendship. The Tovarischi, however, only waved vaguely onwards, which is the only instruction one ever gets in Moscow when one asks the way. On we bumped and jolted and skidded. There was an icy wind blowing and we had no rug. We seemed to cross two rivers, or they may have been river branches. Everything looked very beautiful in the twilight. There was no parapet to the river edge, only some tortuous tree-stems.

Finally we arrived upon the scene to find that some building in a big clearing had burnt to the foundations, and was still burning brightly. Having got out of the car and waded through the mud, I could not get anywhere near, and abandoned the quest. A party of men returning from the fire, surprised at our having a motor, asked Alexandre for his identification papers. Happily he is a member of the Communist party. On the way home he was anxious lest the bad road should cause some damage to the car. If it broke down, he explained cheerfully, there was no other car to be had in these parts, and no telephone to call one up, and it was too far to walk home. It was snowing and we got back at 1 a.m. after losing the way many times.

In the hall I was met by Litvinoff, who, while I was having supper, told me that he had had a message from Trotsky who asked if I would be ready to go off to the front on the morrow at 4 p.m. I had to make up my mind. We discussed the plan in all its aspects. Litvinoff was splendid, he advised me neither way, he merely said he would make all arrangements if I decided to go. I knew that going would involve cold and discomfort and I guessed that I should not really see much of the front, and as the only woman I should be most conspicuous. Yet – what a temptation. Finally about 3 a.m. for various reasons I decided to preserve Trotsky as a memory. Then for the first time Litvinoff said: 'I am so glad.'

OCTOBER 25TH.

Litvinoff was most kind and helped me to move my clay and stand from the Kremlin to the Foreign Office. I would have liked a snapshot of our procession – the moulder carrying the clay block, Litvinoff, in his fur-lined coat and sealskin cap armed with the modelling stand, and I following with the bucket of clay and cloths.

On arrival at the Foreign Office we were greeted by

the Chinese General in uniform and all his staff. Litvinoff, who is likely to be the Soviet representative in China, was rather taken aback by this *rencontre* but the Chinese were enormously amused.

Later, at 9 p.m. I returned with Litvinoff to Tchicherin's office to begin work. While Litvinoff went inside I waited in the secretary's room, and while I was waiting a man hurried through the office. He was a little man in brown trousers and a coat which did not match. With small steps he shuffled hastily along. It might have been a night watchman; it was Tchicherin.

Still I waited, and the length of my wait began to annoy me, and then I began to feel that something was wrong. Presently Litvinoff called me, but I got no further than the doorway.

There Tchicherin confronted me, and in hurried and confused tones said: 'Tonight it is impossible, quite, quite impossible', and disappeared. He had not even allowed me to cross his threshold.

Litvinoff and I looked at each other and walked out. We went upstairs to Litvinoff's office. He was obviously upset and at a perfect loss to explain or excuse. I sat and talked until the car arrived to take me home, and from what Litvinoff said and from what I had seen in that flash, I have learned something of the personality of Tchicherin.

He is an abnormal man, living month after month in that Foreign Office with closed windows and never going out. He insists on having a bedroom there, as he says he has not time to go home to sleep. He works all night, and if a telegram comes in the day he has to be awakened. His nights are days and his days are not entirely nights. He has no idea of time and does not realise that other people live differently. He will ring up a Comrade on the telephone at 3 or 4 o'clock in the morning for the most trivial information. He does all his own work, and will not ring for a secretary or messenger, but runs himself with papers to other departments. He lives on his nerves and the slightest thing throws him off his pivot.

I had been told he was an angel and a saint. What I found was a fluttering and agitated bird. The joke is that he is looked upon as the 'gentleman' of the party. He is by origin well-born and propertied. His property he gave away to the people. Today was a particularly unfortunate one for me. It happened to be the first day for months that Tchicherin had gone out. He went to the dentist. Someone watching him from an office window described to me the phenomenon of Tchicherin in the street. He did not go in a car, but on foot. He stood at the corner of the kerb, looked at the street hesitatingly, much as one might look into a river on a cold day before plunging in. When he did finally decide to get across, he got half way and then ran back. What with the traffic, the fresh air, and the dentist, it must have been a thoroughly unnerving day for him, and no wonder he received me so ill!

OCTOBER 26TH.

Tchicherin sent me a message through Litvinoff, inviting me to start at 4 o'clock in the morning, as that is his quietest time, but it is unfortunately my quietest time too.

OCTOBER 29TH.

I have had four inactive days, but the sense of work completed is a great relief. I am prepared to enjoy the holiday. I have drifted about with Andrev, and in his spare moments with Maxim Litvinoff. On his way to work at midday he first takes me in his car to the place I want to photograph. At 5 o'clock he comes back and has tea with me, brings his portfolio and works in my room till 7. Then he starts out again to meetings. I have interesting talks with him and learn a good deal. He smiles tolerantly when my bourgeois breeding breaks out. But he says I am getting better. Even Rothstein has grown to treat me more seriously.

Today my fourth day of rest began to rouse in me a fresh energy. I long to fill in this interim of waiting with some new work. I have offered to do Litvinoff, and he suggests that I should work in his office; this is so difficult that I have asked him to let me do it at home, in odd moments when he is free. Between the two, nothing gets decided. Meanwhile the sentries at the Kremlin gate have fired my enthusiasm. They are magnificent, wrapped around in goatskin coats with collars that envelop their entire heads. My efforts to get such a one to sit to me have at last been successful.

Andrev and I wandered from building to building this morning to accomplish this purpose. Andrev is great fun to explore with; with a '*Je m'en fiche*' air, he opens all the doors he comes to, and walks in everywhere. I see all sorts of places that I would never dare to investigate alone.

We walked boldly into the barracks; I doubt if a woman had been in before, but I did not attract much attention. A few soldiers gathered round us to hear our explanation to the officer in charge. One or two smiled, the rest looked at me blankly. What Andrev said of course I do not know, except that I understood the officer to ask if we were Bolshevik. Apparently if we were not Bolsheviks we must get permission from the Commandant of the Kremlin before a soldier could be sent to me. Off we went in search of the Commandant. Oh! the dark passages and the stuffy offices; they smelt as if the air belonged to bygone ages. I am sure no fresh air ever leaks in. From there to the military store to obtain an overcoat. They lent me a new one; it was an enormous goatskin. More smells! No living goat ever could have smelt stronger. Andrev, staggering under the weight and the unwieldy size, carried it to my studio to await the soldier's arrival tomorrow. The room reeks of it. My idea is a statuette – only in Russia could one find such a silhouette.

It was still early and I did not want to go home, so we wandered to the Palace, opened more doors, and after a little conversation with some men in an office, one of them took us to see the Museum and the Armoury. This was a great revelation, and I regretted not having seen it before so that I could have had time to go often again. Our guide spoke French, and knew all the things intimately. He talked of them with pride and almost with love. Everything was beautifully arranged. There were glass cases full of Romanoff crowns, jewel studded, and sceptres and harness and trappings set with precious stones. One really got quite dazzled by them. The armour is very fine, I believe, but that I know nothing about and it does not interest me. What I loved were the old coaches. There was one given by Queen Elizabeth of England, the most beautiful bit of painted carving I have ever seen. The French Louis XV and XVI coaches looked vulgar next to it. There was a room full of silver and gold cups. I believe that this contains the finest collection of

English Charles II silver in the world. Moreover so many cups had been collected recently from the churches that there were long wooden trestles covered with them, and they were in process of being catalogued. In the last room were exhibited all the old costumes, church vestments and beautiful brocades. The Coronation robe of Catherine the Great was there, and others that had been wedding and Coronation robes of various other Tsarinas. It is wonderful that these things should have remained unhurt throughout the Revolution.

It is acutely cold, and the river is completely frozen over. Children skate and toboggan everywhere. The side walks have become slides, and are very difficult for the pedestrian who is not equipped with skates. Children here seem to be born able to skate. They strap skates on to any kind of footgear, even on to big, loose felt boots, and they skate everywhere at breakneck speed.

It is a relief not to see people wearily carrying their bundles over their shoulders. Now everyone seems to have put his burden on to a little wooden sledge, and grown-up people look like big children pulling toys on the ends of strings. I have borrowed clothes and Jaegers from my friends. One's nostrils freeze and the breath crystallises on one's fur collar.

The town with its white pall is indescribably beautiful. At dusk the sky is darkened by a flight of grey-backed crows. They settle on the black bare tree branches with the effect of great leaves silhouetted against a coloured evening sky.

At 8.30 this evening, Kameneff unexpectedly walked into my room. It is nearly three weeks since he went to the front. I had almost forgotten about him. He was in tremendous spirits, much thinner, quite unshaved, and with his hair long. He was interesting about the spirit of the Red Army. He says they are wonderfully enthusiastic, and anxious to finish Wrangel and have peace. It is just possible there may be a big *coup* which would obviate a winter campaign.

More than ever do I regret not having gone with Trotsky. They met at Kharkof, and I could have come back with Kameneff.

OCTOBER 31ST.

I went to the Kremlin, and tried to work on my soldier who came to sit to me, but the clay gets so cold and my fingers so numbed, I find I cannot do anything. I built up such a big fire in the stove to keep myself warm, that the unfortunate soldier in the overcoat got nearly apoplectic. Moreover, the hot goatskin smells stronger and stronger. Even the soldier seems to be affected by it. We cannot open the windows and let the cold in. These conditions make work very discouraging. Andrev fetched me at 12.30, and we went to the house of Shucken, who was a cotton-king, and who had the biggest collection of modern French pictures in existence. It is now taken over by the Government, and open on several days a week to the public. Madame Shucken is, I believe, allowed to occupy her rooms in the house. There is no such modern collection in France. There were represented all the artists I have been wanting to see. The first room was full of Claude Monet, and there were three little Whistlers in the doorway leading to a room full of Degas, Renoir, and Cézanne.

Today for the first time I can appreciate Mattisse; there were twenty-one in a room. Next to this was another room containing twenty Gauguins. In a further gallery there was a motley collection, including a couple of Brangwyns, which held their own well. There was also the big William Morris tapestry of Burne-Jones' 'Nativity', which one could hardly bear to look at after the modern French.

Coming out, we passed by a doorway in the snow, rudely painted in blotches of green and yellow; a sentry stood by, and I pointed it out to Andrev who agreed that it was pure Mattisse. One has but to borrow the eyes of another and the same old world appears quite different. I remember that when I had been in Florence a few days, everyone looked like a painted Madonna.

This evening Litvinoff gave a banquet for the departing Chinese General. It was a great event. The dishes as they appeared were like things we have seen in dreams. The party consisted, besides the General and three of his staff, of two interpreters (one being the professor of Chinese at the University of Petrograd), Tchicherin, Karahan, his secretary, Mrs. Karahan, Vanderlip, Rothstein and myself.

We were invited for 9 p.m., but it was half past eleven before we began, true Russian fashion, two hours and a half late. It was for Tchicherin we had to wait: he has no idea of time.

The hours preceding were rather tedious, as conversation through an interpreter is not a success. One Chinaman talked French. He was the President of the Union of Chinese Workers.

Karahan is Armenian; he speaks some strange Eastern language, but nothing that I understand. His wife can only talk Russian. They live in our house, but one seldom sees them as they have their meals in their own apartments. His face is very beautiful, like carved ivory.

He is a great mystery; he lives in a better way than anyone else, smokes the best cigars, drives to his office in a limousine, and looks like the most prosperous gentleman in Europe in his astrachan coat and hat. He must do some very good work for the Government, or he would not be tolerated. I believe Lenin once asked what was the use of him, and he was told that Karahan was most important, for was he not the only man amongst them who could wear evening clothes? Mrs. Karahan was on the stage and is the prettiest woman I have seen in Moscow.

At dinner I sat between the President of the Union of Chinese Workers and Litvinoff, who did host extremely well, and was clever in placing us all. He created so many places of honour that everyone was gratified. He put Tchicherin at the head of the table, so that the General and Vanderlip on either side of him felt that they were guests of honour. He put me on one side of him and Mrs. Karahan at the end of the table opposite Tchicherin.

I ate so many excellent *hors d'oeuvres*, thinking I was never going to eat again, and that nothing else was coming, that I had little room left for what followed. It was a job even to look at a fresh salad and a cauliflower.

Our old manservant was awfully happy. He had on a collar and tie and was washed, and had organised everything beautifully. He had got out the Sèvres salt-cellars, and the cut-glass decanters, and I suppose he just felt that he was back in the old pre-Revolution days and serving his master's friends. He took intense pride in it all.

We had our jokes with him as he went by. Handing me a dish of *boeuf à la mode* he said: '*Magnifique!*' Litvinoff was reprimanded by him for using his knife for his vegetables, and was told that he would not get another. When the apple dumplings came round I was done. I said to the old man: '*Zafter*' (tomorrow). I do hope we shall get some remains. I asked Litvinoff where all the food had come from. He explained to me that there is some food to be had, but that the best is sent to the hospitals and the children.

Then followed speeches. Anything more deplorable to listen to without understanding than Russian being translated into Chinese and *vice versa* is hard to imagine. Tchicherin spoke for quite a long time. The Chinese General's face was immovable. After the Professor had translated, the General replied with much the same sort of face.

After dinner we adjourned to the Karahans' big rooms opposite. Tchicherin was evidently embarrassed at meeting me again. I had no feeling on the subject, and merely laughed.

I said jokingly, 'Comrade Tchicherin, you have treated me very badly.'

He was again quite flustered. Litvinoff told me à propos of Tchicherin that he had advised him to get someone extra into his office to help to get his papers straight. Tchicherin agreed, and said that he had already heard of a young man who would do very well because 'he works during the day, so that he is free at night.' Litvinoff asked when the man should sleep; Tchicherin looked surprised, he had forgotten about that.

NOVEMBER 2ND.

Felt ill. Symptoms of abdominal typhus. Panic on the part of my friends. They say they do not want to lay my body under the Kremlin wall. If they do, I have told them I don't mind speeches, but I would like a prayer. The answer to that was: 'Are you really *croyante*?'

'Well,' I said, 'there are two children praying every night that I may return safe and soon, and the thought of that gives me a certain security.'

'What, you teach your children to pray?'

'But surely they must have something to guide them as they start life?'

'You should teach them reality, and not fantasy.'

'It is not fantasy to believe in a Divine power.'

'You should believe only in your own power.'

That is a conversation I have had as a result of my slight indisposition. It was a conversation that confirms the general idea I have met in others since I have been here. I know these men are idealists and selfless. I did not know these qualities could go hand in hand with atheism.

On this point, Litvinoff corrected me. He did not even want to be regarded as an idealist. That was too unpractical. 'We are idealistic materialists,' he said. To prove their tolerance of religious thought, the churches are all open. But to enter the sacred gateway which leads to the Red Square it was necessary, in pre-Revolution days, for men to pass uncovered. A tablet has now been inserted in the wall engraved with the inscription, 'Religion is the opiate of the people.' Hardly ever have I passed that by without having it pointed out to me with great pride. I never quite understood the spirit of it.

As for the people, they seem to disregard it, to judge by the many who cross themselves as they pass. The shrine seems to be always full of devotees, who pause to pray. The religious feeling of the people will not easily be obliterated and, after all, they need all the comfort and hope they can get, even if the intellectuals do not.

My stay in Russia is nearing its end. Already I see my departure in the near distance. People at home will think I am a Bolshevik, on account of my associations, but I am much too humble to pretend that I understand anything about it.

The more I hear, the clearer it seems to me that economics are the basis of all these arguments, and when it is a question of political economy something happens to my mind, just as it used to when I was a child and had to learn arithmetic. A Bolshevik who can be defeated by argument is not worthy of the name. Therefore I am not a Bolshevik.

But I have tried to understand the spirit of Communism and it interests me overwhelmingly. There are little incidents I like to recall that in no way lessen my love of the people. For example, when the weather began to get cold, before Borodin went away, being unable to explain in Russian what I wanted, I went myself to the back garden to fetch an armload of logs for my fire.

I had to make a long journey through the kitchen, down the corridor and finally through the drawing-room. I have never minded carrying my own wood, but I did think that one of the two men – Borodin who was telephoning, or Boris, who was idling in a Louis XVI chair as I passed through the drawing-room – might have opened the doors for me.

Because they did not I most unforgivably lost my temper, and said I was glad that I was an English woman and not a Russian man. The effect of my attack was different on each of them.

Boris said, 'But it is quite right you should carry your

own wood. Communism means that each should help himself.'

I replied that that was nothing new, that self-help was the oldest deep-rooted feeling in the world, and that if Communism wanted to be original, it must teach the doctrine of helping one another.

Borodin followed me to my room in a state of apology and distress. He brought me two apples and a cigarette, and told me that if I peeled the birch bark off the logs, it made an excellent substitute for kindling. With his advice he did much to help me light my fire. I have never quite made out in my own mind if they were typically Russian or typically Communist. I am still wondering.

I was much laughed at once because I made Vanderlip in the street shoulder a woman's burden and carry it for her to her house. She was a frail well-dressed woman, obviously exhausted by a long walk over cobblestones, and was utterly incompetent to carry the bundle containing her rations. I would have taken it for her myself if I had been alone, but as Vanderlip was champion-in-chief of the frail and the well-dressed, I thought he might as well do it. Litvinoff was amused when he heard about it, and said that one might really find a good deal of work to do in Moscow on those lines.

Vanderlip has told me with great concern that a weak little bourgeoise friend of his, once rich, but now a stenographer, has received a paper ordering her to enlist her services among those who are to shovel the street clear of snow in front of their doors.

'Terrible,' he said.

'Why, terrible?' I asked.

'Terrible that a woman, well-bred and unused to manual labour, should be called upon to shovel snow.'

'But,' I argued, 'she had better food and care when young than the working classes, and ought, therefore, to be physically stronger and more able to do this work than many another.' (I thought of some of my friends in England who made most efficient railway porters during the strike a year ago.)

I said that I should take a pride if I were a Russian bourgeoise in showing people here that I could do as good a day's work as anyone else, and that I was not just useless and helpless as they imagined.

Vanderlip disagreed. He said (and I wonder if it is the American point of view) that women ought not to work at all, they ought to be worked for.

It was quite useless to talk to him about co-operation or the economic independence of women. Besides, it was not about women, it was about Communism that I wanted to talk.

How long and how rambling this is as the result of no occupation and an enforced stay within doors! It is useless to write letters home, and this is a sort of unburdening. I often wonder about my family – whether they are anxious about me (knowing nothing of the peaceful truth), or whether they are too disapproving to be anxious.

I love the bedrock of things here, and the vital energy. If I had no children, I should remain and work. There may be no food for the body, but there is plenty of food for the soul, and I would rather live in discomfort in an atmosphere of gigantic effort, than in luxury among the purposeless. I find I no longer dream of home, and have grown used to conditions which at first seemed hard. I am thankful for the peace which I once mistook for dullness, and appreciate the absence of all the petty tyrannies of civilised life. My mode of living suits me very well. I am glad not to have to take any part in the management of a house. I prefer bad food than to be consulted about it. What the housemaid breaks is not mine, nor any concern of mine. There are no boredoms such as gas bills, taxes, rent and rates, nor Income Tax returns. I never have to sign a cheque, nor to go out with a purse. The obliteration of all social life is a boon. There are no invitations by telephone to accept, refuse, or make decisions about. There is no perplexity about the choice of apparel, nor letters by post that have to be answered. There is leisure to read, leisure to think, leisure to observe. The big ideas, wide horizons and destruction of all the conventions have taken hold of me. Of course I realise that, as a guest of the Government, I am judging things from a personal point of view, and not the point of view of the Russian people. (Few of us are big enough to be purely impersonal.) I like living in this way. It may seem a strange taste to those people who have the sense of possession, the collectors' instinct, or the love of home. I have none of these; so long as I have a place to work in, and plenty of work to do, and leisure in which to think about it, I ask little more.

My ear has accustomed itself to the language of Communism, I have forgotten the English of my own world. I do not mean that I am a Communist, nor that I think it is a practical theory, perhaps it is not, but it seems to me, nevertheless, that the Russian people get gratis a good many privileges, such as education, lodging, food, railways, theatres, even postage, and a standard wage thrown in. If the absence of prosperity is marked, the absence of poverty is remarkable. The people's sufferings are chiefly caused by lack of food, fuel and clothing.

This is not the fault of the Government. The Soviet system does not do it to spite them, or because it enjoys their discomfiture. Only peace with the world can ameliorate their sufferings, and Russia is not at war with the world, the world is at war with Russia. Why am I happy here, shut off from all I belong to? What is there about this country that has always made everyone fall under its spell? I have been wondering. My mind conjures up English life and English conditions, and makes comparisons. Why are these people, who have so much less education, so much more cultured than we are? The galleries of London are empty. In the British Museum one meets an occasional German student. Here the galleries and museums are full of working people. London provides revues and plays of humiliating mediocrity, which the educated classes applaud and enjoy. Here the masses crowd to see Shakespeare. At Covent Garden it is the gallery that cares for music, and the boxes are full of weary fashion, which arrives late and talks all the time. Here the houses are overcrowded with workers and peasants who listen to the most classical operas. Have they only gone as someone might with a new sense of possession to inspect a property they have suddenly inherited? Or have they a true love of the beautiful and a real power of discrimination? These are the questions I ask myself. Civilisation has put on so many garments that one has trouble in getting down to reality. One needs to throw off civilisation and to begin anew, and begin better, and all that is required is just courage. What Lenin thinks about nations applies to individuals. Before reconstruction can take place there must be a revolution to obliterate everything in one that existed before. I am appalled by the realisation of my upbringing and the futile view-point instilled into me by an obsolete class tradition. Time is the most valuable material in the world, and there at least we all start equally, but I was taught to scatter mine thoughtlessly, as though it were infinite. Now for the first time I feel morally and mentally free, and yet they say there is no freedom here. If a paper pass or an identification card hampers one's freedom, then it is true. There may be restrictions to the individual, and if I were a Russian subject I might not be allowed to leave the country, but I seem to have been obliged to leave England rather clandestinely.

Freedom is an illusion, there really is not any in the world except the freedom one creates intellectually for oneself.

My work is ended, but I am loth to go. I love this place and all the people in it. I love the people I have met, and the people who pass by me in the street. I love the atmosphere laden with melancholy, with sacrifice, with tragedy. I am inspired by this Nation, purified by Fire. I admire the dignity of their suffering and the courage of their belief.

I should like to live among them for ever, or else work for them outside, work and fight for the Peace that will heal their wounds.

NOVEMBER 5TH.

A message has arrived at third hand from Kalinin, offering to sit to me. He promised to a long time ago before he went to the front. He got back from the front on October 30th, with Kameneff, and had he given me the chance then there would have been plenty of time. Now everything is settled for me to go tomorrow with

Professor Lomonosoff in his special train. I am very disappointed, Kalinin has a head that interests me. I have wanted to do a Russian peasant type, and he is one. But if I do not get away in Lomonosoff's train I may delay a long time. England seems so very far away, and the children will think I have forgotten them. Perhaps if I could work without my fingers getting frozen I would stop and do him, and do Litvinoff too. But I have made a failure of my soldier, and it is not encouraging. An appointment was made for me with Kalinin at 1 o'clock to see him in his office. Litvinoff kindly took me there. It was in some building facing the Kremlin. We went in and after some searching and inquiry, found the outer rooms of his office. There seemed to be two or three of these, and they were full of people sitting on benches round the wall. Some looked miserable, and were curled up in a heap with shawls over their heads, others were sleeping in corners, or huddled up by the stove. They spat on the floor, smoked and were perfectly silent. These were all people who came with a grievance to lay before their President. Litvinoff, when he went in, asked whether it was Kalinin's office – a nod and a grunt assented that it was. Litvinoff, who is impatient, went from room to room, but we could find no trace of Kalinin. Finally he opened a door that proved to be the private office, and a short-haired girl secretary looked up and said Kalinin might return in half an hour. So he might, but with an experience of Russian official appointments, it seemed likely that he might not appear for a couple of hours. We left messages and retreated. On our way out someone, rousing himself from a corner, asked whether Kalinin was really in his room or not. Perhaps they thought we were privileged people, while they were kept waiting; I was rather glad that we could say he was not there. I came away with a melancholy impression of the place, but Kalinin, with his kindly face, must be the best sort of man to whom the people can tell their troubles.

We then drove to the statue of Dostoievsky, which is a beautiful bit of work in granite and which I wanted to photograph. In the same square there is another granite statue by the same artist, which is usually known as 'The Thinker'. It is, if anything, better than the Dostoievsky.

From there I went to the Kremlin to see how the packing of my heads was progressing. I was surprised to find that the wooden cases had been delivered, owing, no doubt, to the combined efforts of Kameneff, Litvinoff, Andrev, and my kind Comrade Unachidse, from whom all blessings flow. Moreover the heads were packed, so that there was nothing for me to do. I said good-bye very sadly to my nice moulder, whom I like so much. He is intelligent, well-mannered, and efficient. He bent down and kissed my hand with the simplicity and dignity of a prince. I gave him a woollen jersey, as he feels the cold, and with all his thousands of roubles that he earns he cannot buy such a thing. I gave one last look round the grim room to which I have become attached, and, with a lump in my throat, departed down the long stone passage, through which my footsteps re-echoed for the last time.

Then I crossed the courtyard and went to lunch at the Kremlin table d'hôte. This table d'hôte, which is the Communist restaurant reserved for all the Commissars and workers in the Kremlin, was unusually full today. I was lucky to get my place. Lunarcharsky sat opposite me. He has just returned to Moscow and I regretted there was no one present who could introduce us.

STATUE OF DOSTOIEVSKY

My neighbours observed me reading an English guide-book to the Kremlin, and attempted odd bits of conversation, but their English completely broke down. It is a great loss not being able to understand a word of Russian, as the conversation at the long table was very animated and must have been interesting.

The interest for me was in the faces of the men themselves, who were of the most varied type it would be possible to collect. One could not say they were typically Russian or typical of any race or of any particular character, and yet there was some invisible link that bound all these men together in one common thought.

After lunch Andrev fetched me, and an official showed us all over the Tsar's palace. There were exquisite small rooms with vaulted ceilings and frescoed walls, from which it was evident that the stage scenery in the Russian operas had been copied. There were still traces of red bunting and appeals to the workers of the world to unite in the colossal room, over-decorated with gold, which was the Throne Room of the Romanoffs, and in which the Third International had its last meeting.

The modern apartments in the new wing are bad architecture and in bad taste, but everything is left undisturbed. Even the photographs of the Tsar's Coronation are still hanging in their frames in some of the rooms. The Royal Family scarcely came to Moscow, so that the place must have always had an uninhabited feeling. One did not feel the ghosts of former times as in some of the older parts of the building.

My last evening was spent with Andrev, Litvinoff and Kameneff, who came and sat in my room. Kameneff brought me a sheepskin hat, such as I had seen at the Sukharefski market and wanted so much, also the £100

I had entrusted to his care when we started, which I have
never had occasion to spend. He then told me that my
departure was most ill-timed. Tomorrow is the eve of the
Anniversary of the Revolution. There are going to be
great celebrations. A big meeting will be held at the
Opera House, at which Lenin and Trotsky are going to
speak. It is only on very rare occasions that Lenin
appears in public, and it would be interesting to hear
him. The meeting is called for 4 o'clock, but it will be
three or four hours late, and my train leaves at 8. If only
Lomonosoff would delay his train I could attend. The
next day, on the 7th, there will be a ball, and on the 8th
a banquet at our house for the Foreign Office. Moreover,
the Entente papers promise a *coup d'état* for the 7th and
Litvinoff suggested that I should wait and 'see the show'.
But I know by experience that I should only wait in vain.
When I was alone with Kameneff he said to me: 'Well,
did I keep my promises?' I told him that everything had
been fulfilled, and had exceeded even my expectations.
I told him I was overwhelmed by the kindness I had
received 'considering I am an enemy Englishwoman'. He
would not listen to any words of appreciation, he smiled
in his genial, kindly way: 'Of course we were glad to
receive you, and to have you among us, *une femme
artiste*, what did it matter to us, your nationality, or your
relations. There is only one thing, *que nous ne pouvons
pas supporter*', and for the first time in all the months I
have known him, a hard look passed over his face, and
he set his teeth: 'The only thing we cannot stand *c'est
l'espionage*', and the way he said it gave me a shiver
down my spine. It was only a passing shadow, and the
next moment he was telling me that he really regarded
me as a woman of courage for coming just on his word,

153

adding that when he saw me on the departure platform 'with two small hand-bags, I knew in that moment that you were not any ordinary woman!' We looked back on our London days and laughingly discussed the first sitting when he invited me to come to Moscow. I told him 'I did not believe that you were serious when you asked me', and he said, 'Neither did I believe you were serious when you accepted.' He then proceeded to outline for me exactly what the effect of my Moscow visit would have on my friends, on my family, in the Press, and on my career. His accuracy remains to be seen.

NOVEMBER 6TH.

Off at last – what a hectic day. Litvinoff telephoned to me in the morning from the Commissariat to say that my big wooden cases (my coffins I call them, they are the same shape) were going to be conveyed from my studio to the station, and that I need not concern myself about them. It was not until midday that I learnt for certain that Professor Lomonosoff was going to start tonight. In Russia one makes no plans, things happen when they happen! With a rashness that nearly proved reckless, I distributed my few belongings among my friends. To a lady doctor friend of Andrev who had been nice to me, I left all my stockings, a box of soap, a skirt, a jersey and my cloth overcoat. To the maids in the house, my shoes and goloshes, workbag, jersey, fur-lined dressing jacket, pair of gloves, and hat. To Rothstein, as a parting gift, my hot-water bottle and medicine case. I started on my journey in the clothes I stood up in. The maids, to my intense embarrassment, kissed my hands and nearly wept. I nearly kissed them in return. I started off with Litvinoff, and Rothstein came to the front door to see the last of me. He overwhelmed me with compliments: 'You have been a brick, you have played up splendidly, you have never complained.' I tried to explain that I hadn't played up, and that I had not been anything except very happy. I might have added that living Communistically had proved to me that one must either love or hate the people one sees every day for any length of time. Hate may be tempered into dislike, and Love may be more appropriately termed friendship or affection, but it was certainly affection that I had grown to feel for Rothstein. He seemed somehow to belong to our environment, we should have missed him if he hadn't been there. Just occasionally he said things about England that roused opposition in me. I feel about England as most people do about their relations, that I may abuse my own, but no one else may. I realised, when I got to know him better, that his attitude was not so much one of hostility to England as of intense pride in Russia, and so I forgave him. During my first days in Moscow, Rothstein unfailingly cross-questioned me at supper as to how I had spent my day, where I had lunched, whom I had seen, and what time I had come home. At last I said to him: 'Don't ask me, try and find out', and I chaffed him so that he has to give up asking. I never knew whether there was a motive in his curiosity or not. At all events, he never was anything but a kindly and helpful friend to me. I drove away from No. 14, Sofiskaya Naberezhnaya in an open car in the bright light of a full moon, glittering stars, and hard frost. Litvinoff, observing that I looked back at it rather sentimentally, said: 'That is your Moscow home, the next time you come you will bring your children', and I felt that I did not look upon it for the last time. We drove first to the Commissariat for Foreign

Affairs, as he had some packages of papers to pick up there which he had taken away in the morning to have sealed up for me. I waited outside in the car for some time. When he rejoined me he was agitated, my 'coffins', he had just learnt, were still at the Kremlin. Organisation had miscarried, it was 'somebody's' fault. The lorry had waited for them three hours, but the sentry at the building had refused to deliver them up. What could have happened? Everyone was at the big Opera House meeting, so all telephoning efforts to get hold of responsible help had been in vain. We had three-quarters of an hour before the train was due to start. I suggested driving to the Kremlin to see what we could do. Happily I still had my pass on me, so we got in by the sentry. The building, ever before so busy, was now utterly deserted and resonant. I unlocked the door of my studio, and there were the two coffins lying packed and sealed and unmoved. I lifted one end of one, it was far beyond our combined strengths to carry, and the motor could not have taken them. We gave it up in despair. Down in the courtyard our car refused to move, the chauffeur was tinkering at it. It seemed to have a real congested chill. Train time was drawing near. The station was some way off. 'Stay,' said Litvinoff. I had visions of staying, perhaps indefinitely, having parted with all except what I stood up in.

I looked round at the beloved Kremlin, to which I had already said good-bye not expecting to see it again. It seemed more beautiful than ever, more still, more dignified, more impassive. The clock in the old Spassky tower complainingly chimed three times, it was a quarter to seven. At last the car breathed, pulsed, started, then stopped. Then pulsed, grunted, and started again.

We were off, and, as the road lay down hill, it seemed possible that the car, which was misfiring badly, might just get there. It seemed to be an evening of mishaps, and I felt fated not to leave Moscow. However, we reached the station at exactly 7, and I gathered up all I could in each hand, and ran towards a crowd that stood by the only train in the station. Litvinoff shouted to me 'You needn't run.' Indeed, I need not, as the only train in the station was not the train of Professor Lomonosoff. His special came in at another platform about half an hour later, and never went out till after 9. Had we known, something could have been done in the time to get the cases to the train, also I could have gone to the meeting and heard Lenin. No one was more frantic than Lomonosoff, who prided himself on his train being punctual. But it could not be helped, the train had just returned from the Urals, and was in a state of disorder.

Litvinoff, when he said good-bye to me, promised to send on my cases by courier to Reval in time to catch the Stockholm boat. He then aroused my curiosity by telling me that he had been a better friend to me than I should ever know. I begged him to explain, but he said that I must wait ten years or so.

NOVEMBER 7TH. *In the train.*

Professor Lomonosoff is the Minister of Railways. We are carrying six and a half million pounds in gold, which he is taking to Germany to buy locomotives. We are accompanied by an armed guard.

We were held up many hours last night because there was an accident on the line and it took a long time to clear. Periodically the axle of the gold car breaks, or the oil-box takes fire, and we stop perpetually: but we are steadily nearing our goal. It really does not matter how long we take so long as we catch next Thursday's boat from Reval.

Besides Lomonosoff's staff, which he is taking with him to Germany, our party consists of Vanderlip and Neuroteva, and a charming man called D—, who is a railway expert. He was once a very rich man and in the Tsar's entourage. He seemed anxious to tell me as quickly as possible that he was a Monarchist, as if to be mistaken for a Bolshevik were more than he could bear. He looked anaemic and well bred, with deep-set, sad eyes and a calm and resignation that were almost tragic.

He differed bitterly and openly in his views from Lomonosoff, and said: 'I am a Russian. I am working for Russia, not for the Bolsheviks', and then called them robbers. Professor Lomonosoff sat back in his chair and chuckled. He said: 'You call us robbers, but we called you robbers.' It was just a question of which robber came out on top.

Afterwards, when Lomonosoff left us, I begged D— not to indulge in any more political discussions. 'I shall be over the frontier in a few hours, but you have to live here. Do take heed for yourself.'

He shrugged his shoulders. 'One dies but once,' he said, laughing, and then explained: 'They know my views well, but I can do good work for them, and they know that I am not in touch with counter-Revolutionary movements, and that I take no part in politics, so I am safe enough.'

Lomonosoff, who had been a railway official in Tsarist days, told us how he had accompanied the Tsar's train to Tsarskoe-Selo. The Tsar, he said, had even up to that moment not realised the meaning of the Revolution. He probably thought he was retiring to Siberia until the storm had blown over. At the station, on his arrival, his bodyguard had by courtesy been drawn up to greet him. The Tsar alighted from the train, and went to inspect the guard with the usual greeting: 'Good health to you, soldiers!' The answer is: 'Good health to your Imperial Majesty', but on this occasion the soldiers answered almost with one voice, 'Good health to you, Colonel!' The Tsar seemed to realise for the first time the real situation. He became ashen white, turned the collar of his overcoat up, and shrank away.

Lomonosoff also gave us a vivid and thrilling account of the detailed organisation, in which he took part, with the purpose of wrecking the Tsar's train while he was on his way to Siberia. Two runaway engines were to be despatched with no one on board to collide with the back of the Tsar's train. These plans were only frustrated at the last second by news of the Tsar's abdication.

When he proceeded to tell us how the Tsar's entourage deserted him as rats do a sinking ship, it was evidently very painful to D— who sat grimly silent. I could not help feeling that they enjoyed his discomfiture a little bit.

Later, when we were again alone together, he said to me rather passionately: 'It is not true that everyone deserted my Tsar, for my best friend followed him to Siberia to share his death, and there were devoted friends of the Tsarina who did the same.'

We are now nearing the frontier. The little country stations, decorated for the 7th with red bunting and pictures of Lenin, will soon be passed. Back we go to the old world of tips and restaurants and civilisation.

Good-bye, wonder world, good-bye – good-bye!

NOVEMBER 12TH. *Reval, Esthonia.*

We arrived in Reval late on Tuesday night, the 9th. I was handed a package containing my two volumes of diary and all my kodak films, which thanks to Litvinoff had been sealed with Government seals and confided to a courier who kept them in his charge until we were over the frontier.

I have written my diary all these weeks as trustingly as though I were in my own home, never foreseeing any difficulties of departure. My trust in Providence is always justified.

The next day I went to the British Consulate. Mr. Leslie (no relation) made me extremely welcome. He said that he had heard of me from H. G. Wells, and that until then he had not known I was in Russia: I had (reproachfully) not addressed myself to the Consulate on my ingoing journey. I found that he had a Henry James cult, and had read everything Henry James had written, including the two volumes of letters. He gave me his bathroom for an hour and a half, invited me to luncheon and then arranged for me to stay the remaining two days in Reval with a most hospitable English couple, Mr. and Mrs. Harwood, who lived in a beautiful villa on the seashore. There I was overwhelmed by kindness.

I also learned with some curiosity and interest the politics of Esthonia, the half-Bolshevik conditions of things, and the history of the Baltic Germans, their settlement in Reval and their forced departure. It is an amusing but complicated little side-show.

During my stay in Reval I had to go several times to the Soviet headquarters at the Hotel Petersbourg. It amuses me to recall my bewildered impression of last September. This time when I went I felt thoroughly at home. Not only did Comrade Gai take a great deal of trouble for me, but Gukovski received me as a friend.

On Thursday morning the coffins arrived from Moscow by courier, as promised by Litvinoff, and I had a fine game of dodge. Gai sent them on a lorry to me at the British Consulate just when I had left, and they returned to the Hotel Petersbourg while I was chasing after them to the British Consulate. Finally I got them down to the quay, but they were not allowed on board because there was not the required official paper from Moscow. Had the ship left as she was supposed to leave at midday, they certainly would not have been on board, but there was a storm brewing so the ship delayed sailing a day. When Gai had finally sent me the necessary paper, I sought out the Captain and begged him to have my cases put somewhere especially safe. 'They contain the heads of Lenin and Trotsky,' I exclaimed. The Captain looked awfully impressed and pleased, so pleased that I added 'plaster heads – and breakable'.

'A plaster head of Trotsky – and breakable? Come on! let us break Trotsky's head', and he made towards it threateningly, much to the amusement of the onlookers.

My departure from Reval was most carefully and kindly superintended by my late Bolshevik hosts, whose representatives in Reval and also Professor Lomonosoff and his staff did everything in their power to be kind and attentive.

We are on our way now to Stockholm. I find the same Swedish banker, Mr. Aschberg, on board who went across with us in September. He is in charge of a cabin full of gold. He takes good care of me and I am glad to find a friend. I am told the food on board is very bad, but I think it is marvellous.

NOVEMBER 16TH. *Stockholm, Sweden.*

I have lost all track of time. Storms forced our little boat to anchor under the shelter of an Aland isle for two days and a night.

On our arrival late at night at Stockholm we were met by Professor Lomonosoff's representative with a car, and after we had all been submitted to a search, not for arms, but for insects, and declared fit to step on to Swedish soil, I was whirled off to the Hotel Anglais.

I had fully expected to be lost and forgotten on leaving Moscow, but here I am being taken care of in the third country away. If the Stockholm experiences foreshadow my coming reception in England, it promises to be hectic. I am not allowed breathing space, nor eating space.

Reporters besiege me. They even walk up to my room without being announced. I am so ignorant of the papers they represent that I say all the wrong things. One paper, a Conservative one, says that I declared Trotsky to be a perfect gentleman. This, if it gets back to Moscow, is most embarrassing. Never in my wildest moments would I use so mediocre a description to apply to Trotsky. I might say he was a genius, a superman, or a devil. Anyway, in Russia we talk of men and women and not of ladies and gentlemen. I dare say that the editor meant well, and that things get distorted in translation.

The experience of returning through Stockholm is rather unique. Because we have both come out of Russia together, Mr. Vanderlip and I have been entertained at the same parties, but for me Frederick Ström and the Russian Bolsheviks are invited and for Vanderlip the leading Swedish bankers. It is a queer amalgamation, but it works well.

The first evening I talked to Socialist Ström and a

Conservative banker for an hour and a half in flowing but execrable German. They did not laugh at my grammar, but listened and spurred me on with questions. The German of my childhood slightly practised in Moscow has returned to me with a rush.

I have been invited to do a monument for a public square in Stockholm representing Peace uniting the workers of the Right and Left Wings. The money has been subscribed in kroner by the workpeople. It is an international thing, and they would be pleased if I would do it. It is a subject which rather lends itself to allegorical treatment and appeals to the imagination.

I am now in the night train for Göteborg. Before I left I went to tea with the children at the Palace. The Crown Prince unfortunately was in Rome. The children seemed lonely, but well. Princess Ingred looked sad, big-eyed and rather pale. The baby, Johnny, is adorable. He is a thing so sweet to woman, so much to be appreciated. One feels the maternal spirit-arms round him.

I also went to see the Comptroller of the Queen's household, an artist and an old friend of many years. Here the impression I received of prejudice against my Russian friends was overwhelming, but I suppose, in Court circles, this is to be expected.

NOVEMBER 18TH. *Göteborg to Newcastle.*

More delays, owing to storms. Always there are delays on this journey, do what one will it is impossible to hurry. In pre-war days it took two days to come from Russia. Now it takes two weeks.

NOVEMBER 23RD. *London.*

We arrived at Newcastle at midnight on the 19th. Steaming up the Tyne at night is wonderful, all the arc lights throwing into relief great machinery and construction. The activity and work looked colossal. How can Russia fight this iron industrialism? As soon as we had glided alongside the quay, and I had touched English soil once more, I was not left in doubt one moment as to the truth of Kameneff's premonitions.

While the coffins were being opened with chisel and hammer at the Custom House, reporters, who declared they had come from London and had been waiting two days, clamoured for information. The head official of the Customs was very abrupt in his manner and subjected all my luggage to a most ruthless search. I did not declare the identity of my heads, but from the unpleasant official attitude I guessed that they were already known. One official began examining a large album of photographs. I said to him: 'That isn't contraband, they are photographs of my work; yes, that one is Mr. Churchill, if it interests you, you may look at it.' He nearly flung it down. 'I've no scent and no tobacco, one doesn't get those things in Russia,' I said. Unfortunately at that minute he came upon a packet of Soviet cigarettes, my last ration that I had carefully kept and brought back to England. But he said: 'That is not what we are looking for.' Whatever he was looking for he didn't find.

He then poked his arm up to the elbow in the straw and shavings that wrapped up Dzhirjinsky, until satisfied that it was not a Christmas bran pie. I then got it nailed down again, and accepted the newspaper reporters' invitation to drive with them from the quay to the station. There another man met me armed with a kodak and a flashlight. I sympathise with professional keenness, but I will not be butchered to make a Roman holiday. The moment seemed inappropriate. There were inebriated young fellows shouting, singing, and falling about the stations to such an extent that the policeman, who had vainly tried to look the other way, had finally to take notice, but he had to knock one of them down before he could arrest him. It was a revolting sight to which one had grown unaccustomed. I was glad to get into my sleeper and shut out the sight and sound of Newcastle at midnight.

Since then my soul, my life, my time, has been no longer my own. I have been pursued, besieged, harassed, feasted, attacked, appraised in turn.

I have seen the anti-Bolshevik in all his glory of prejudice, hate and bitterness.

The Bolshevik is a new phenomenon, but the anti-Bolshevik is merely history repeating itself. We read of the same condition of mind in England after the Napoleonic wars; the same fear of French Revolutionary ideas, and same action and reactions.

Yet, if people would only realise it, Revolutions are not caused by propaganda, nor by plots. In Russia the Revolution failed every time it was organised. It was brought about by cause and effect at the very moment when the present leaders were in exile in the four corners of the globe.

Alexinsky says in his *Modern Russia*: 'Seek for the cause of Revolution neither in the ardent propaganda of the Revolutionists nor in the bad qualities of monarchs and their advisers, but in the deep and silent operation of certain forces, which lead new social classes upon the stage of history.' It is futile to waste hate upon these forces, or to call them Lenin and Trotsky, when really it is the law of evolution and change that is demonstrating in certain parts of the earth.

NOTES

I have adopted the modern standard transliterations of Russian names. *M.A.*

Page 7. Kameneff and Krassin. Lev Borisovich Kamenev (born Rosenfeld, 1883–1936) was one of Lenin's leading comrades. He was exiled from Tsarist Russia and returned to the country with Lenin from Zurich in 1917 after the fall of Nicholas II. After Lenin's death, Kamenev allied with Stalin and Zinoviev against Trotsky. Both Kamenev and Zinoviev found themselves 'dropped from the leading car' by Stalin and eventually were destroyed by him, being shot together on the same day in 1936.

Leonid Borisovich Krassin (1870–1926) was a revolutionary terrorist in Russia before 1914: one of his bombs in 1906 cost the legs of the daughter of Stolypin, the last effective minister of Nicholas II. He was an early rival of Lenin for the leadership of the Bolshevik Party, but after 1917 he was entrusted with important posts dealing with foreign affairs and trade. He was an early advocate of the idea that the Soviet economy should be run by managers chosen for their competence rather than their ideological zeal – an idea grudgingly taken up in the late 1980s! Krassin was later the Soviet Commissar for Trade and, before formal diplomatic relations were opened between Britain and Soviet Russia, used the argument that business with Russia would help reduce unemployment and lift British firms out of the post-war recession. He died as first Soviet Ambassador in London in 1926.

Page 11. Chaliapin. Feodor Ivanovich Chaliapin (1873–1938) –

the greatest Russian bass of his generation. Despite attempts by the Soviet regime to curry favour with him, he fled the country in 1921 and died in French exile, but the Soviet Union later arranged for him to be exhumed and reburied in his homeland despite his rejection of Communism.

Page 14. Lansbury. George Lansbury (1859–1940) – leader of the Labour Party, 1931–35. A lifelong pacifist, Lansbury discredited himself by naively visiting Hitler and Mussolini in 1937 in the hope of convincing them to adopt his ideals.

Page 16. Polish success over the Red Army. Soviet Russia and Poland were at war from 1919 to 1921. The defeat of the Red Army at the gates of Warsaw in August 1920 dashed any hopes of an immediate worldwide Communist revolution spread by Trotsky's 'armed missionaries'. Stalin's insubordination during the campaign was one of the causes of the catastrophe and was a key event in his vendetta against Trotsky which culminated in Trotsky's murder by Stalin's agent, Ramon Mercador, in Mexico twenty years later.

Page 18. F. E. F. E. Smith, Lord Birkenhead (1872–1930). Despite his failure to enter Harrow, academic success laid the foundations of a dazzling career (newspaper reports of which he sent to the hapless headmaster of Harrow until his death). The leading young barrister of his generation, Smith entered Parliament as one of the fiercest opponents of Irish Nationalism on the Conservative benches. Despite an early antagonism to Churchill, he joined him as a leading opponent of any diminution of the British Empire and his wit could be cruel but was no respecter of persons: when Judge Willis objected to Smith's condescending tone, asking, 'What do you think I am on the bench for, Mr Smith?', he replied, 'It is not for me to attempt to fathom the inscrutable workings of Providence.' He famously used the Athenaeum's lavatory *en route* through St James's: asked by the porter if he was a member of the Club, he retorted, 'Club as well, is it?' Drank himself to death.

Page 19. Tchicherin. Georgi Vasiliyevich Chicherin (1872–1936), bourgeois by origin, became Foreign Commissar after Trotsky's brief period in office. Chicherin opened diplomatic relations with the outside world, most notably with Germany, the other pariah state after the First World War. After retiring on grounds of ill health and being replaced by Litvinov (see below), Chicherin spent his last years writing about the music of Mozart. He died in his bed.

Page 22. Dzhirjinsky. Feliks Edmundovich Dzerzhinsky (1877–1926), a Polish nobleman by birth, rejected nationalism as the natural means of opposing the Tsarist Russian domination of Poland and became a Bolshevik. After the revolution, he became the first head of the Soviet secret police, the Cheka (the Extraordinary Commission for the Struggle against Counter-revolution and Sabotage). An ascetic fanatic, described in official propaganda as the 'Knight of the Proletariat', Dzerzhinsky's main concern apart from liquidating the class enemy was care for the growing number of orphans in Soviet Russia – many of whom he recruited into the ranks of his Chekists, i.e. the cause of their bereavement. A supporter of Stalin in the future leader's struggle for power against Trotsky, Kamenev and Zinoviev, Dzerzhinsky conveniently died of 'overwork' after their defeat. On 23rd August 1991 his statue outside the Lubyanka in Moscow, the headquarters of the KGB, was the first Soviet idol to be symbolically toppled after the failure of the coup organised by his successor, Kryuchkov.

Maxim Gorki. Maxim Gorky (1868–1936) – one of Russia's leading twentieth-century writers and an early sympathiser with Marxism. Despite his willingness to make propaganda on behalf of the regime, he preferred to live abroad, especially in Capri. Enticed back to the Soviet Union by Stalin, he was critical of the human suffering inflicted in the 1930s and died mysteriously, possibly poisoned.

Page 28. Wrangel. General Pyotr Nikolayevich Wrangel (1878–1928) – the last leader of the Whites in the Civil War. Although he evacuated his troops from the Crimea in 1920, he remained an object of hostile Soviet propaganda long after his death in Belgrade.

Page 33. Lord Mayor of Cork. Terence MacSwiney went on

hunger-strike against British rule in Ireland, eventually dying after seventy-four days. (The Bobby Sands of his day.)

Page 34. Litvinoff. Maxim Litvinov (1876–1952) was an early Bolshevik and later an outstanding Soviet diplomat. He was Commissar for Foreign Affairs from 1930 to 1939. Litvinov was widely travelled and unlike some of his post-revolutionary comrades he avoided self-consciously anti-bourgeois bad manners in his dealings with Westerners. Under a cloud during the Nazi–Soviet Pact because of his Jewish origins, Litvinov returned to high diplomatic office after 1941. Despite his fears of imminent arrest in the anti-Semitic persecution of Stalin's last years, Litvinov died in his bed.

Page 35. Mrs Litvinoff – Ivy Low (1889–1977), English-born wife of the future Soviet Foreign Commissar who survived him and returned to live out her old age in Hove.

Page 38. Rjasanoff – possibly the editor of the Russian edition of the collected works of Marx and Engels.

Page 47. Yudenitch. General Nikolai Nikolayevich Yudenich (1862–1933), commander of the White armies in north-western Russia.

Page 49. Zinoviev. Grigori Yevseyevich Zinoviev (1883–1936), a leading Bolshevik in the Comintern (the international Communist movement), regarded himself as Lenin's natural successor. A bitter rival of Trotsky, Zinoviev helped Stalin to defeat the Commissar for War in the power struggle after Lenin's death, only to be done down in his turn. Always closely associated with Kamenev. Stalin had them shot together and enjoyed the executioner's impersonation of their last moments: Zinoviev rhetorically denouncing his murderers while Kamenev preferred silence.

Mrs Philip Snowden – wife of the first Labour Chancellor of the Exchequer and an early and brief fellow-traveller. Philip Snowden (1864–1937) soon lost any sympathy with revolutionary Russia. He joined Ramsay MacDonald in breaking with Labour in the crisis of 1931 and allying with Baldwin's Tories. During the

1931 general election campaign, Snowden used one of the first party political broadcasts to denounce Labour's policies as 'Bolshevism run mad'.

Page 54. Serge Trotsky – son of Lev Trotsky and another of Stalin's future victims.

Page 57. John Reed (1887–1920) – son of a US judge who became a radical journalist covering the Mexican Revolution in 1916–17 before travelling to Russia after the February Revolution. His *Ten Days that Shook the World* (1919) was a romantic account of Lenin's seizure of power in October (modern-style November) 1917. Reed became active in the Comintern as one of its leading international propagandists. In August 1920 he contracted typhoid after eating a contaminated water melon in Baku where he was a delegate to the Comintern's Congress of the Peoples of the East intended to promote revolution in Asia. He was one of the first Communist heroes to be buried in the Kremlin wall, Dzerzhinsky being one of the pall-bearers – just one of many facts elided out of *Reds*, Warren Beatty's memorably inaccurate film of Reed's life with Louise Bryant.

Page 58. Rosenfeld – Kamenev's brother, a painter.

Mr Rothstein – probably the future censor of press reports by foreign journalists based in Moscow.

Mr W. B. Vanderlip – 'Washington B. Vanderlip, Jr' was a con-man who flitted briefly across the Soviet stage in late 1920. Lenin mistook him for a Vanderbilt and hoped to use the self-proclaimed billionaire's contacts with the freshly elected Republican President, Warren Harding, to open trade and diplomatic relations with the United States.

Page 66. Comrade Unachidse. Yenachidse, an Armenian Communist who committed suicide under Stalin.

Page 67. Clara Zetkin (1857–1933) – a leading German Marxist and founder of the German Communist Party. Unlike Kollontai (see below) she had old-fashioned tastes in dress, men and music. Died in exile in the Soviet Union.

Mme Kolontai. Alexandra Kollontai (1872–1952), leading Bolshevik feminist and proponent of free love. Lenin quashed demands for a death sentence against her at the end of the Civil War, although she had allowed an affair to distract her from her duties. Spent much of the next thirty years as a Soviet diplomat, most importantly in Sweden during the Second World War. One of the few Old Bolsheviks to die under Stalin in her own bed.

Page 72. Millerand. Alexandre Millerand (1859–1943), the first socialist to take office in a Western government in France in 1899. He was derided by all Marxist true believers like Lenin as a reformist ever afterwards, not least for reducing the length of the working day and establishing minimum wages for public employees. He was President of France, 1920–24.

Page 74. Michael Borodin. Mikhail Markovitch Borodin (1884–1951), born Gruzenberg. A legend in his own lifetime as the Comintern's leading agent in China in the 1920s. After Stalin's consolidation of power, he was demoted to the position of editor of *Moscow News*, the newspaper for foreigners, in 1932. He disappeared in February 1949 as Stalin's 'anti-cosmopolitan' purge got under way and died in a Siberian camp two years later.

Page 76. Bucharin and Bela Kun. Nikolai Ivanovich Bukharin (1888–1938). Lenin called him the 'darling of the Party'. Purged under Stalin, he was chief defendant at the last great show trial and executed afterwards.

Bela Kun (1886–1939?). Led the short-lived Soviet Republic of Hungary in 1919. Escaped after its collapse to the Soviet Union, where he played a leading role in the Comintern until he disappeared in 1937 during Stalin's purges. This did not stop the post-war Communist rulers of his native Hungary from naming many streets after him, but the names have now been changed, leaving him in oblivion once more.

Page 89. H. G. Wells arrived. Wells gave a less than flattering portrait of Lenin, who freely admitted his cynical exploitation of the Russian peasantry to him in that bitterest of winters, 1920–21, when he still hoped to replace free farming with state-run collectives: 'We have in places large-scale agriculture,' Lenin told Wells. 'It can be extended first to one province, then another. The peasants of the other provinces, selfish and illiterate, will not know what is happening until their turn comes!' Wells recorded: 'At the mention of the peasant, Lenin's head came nearer mine; his manner became confidential. As if after all the peasant might overhear.'

Page 94. Monsieur Churchill. Winston Spencer Churchill (1874–1965). Cousin of the author. Leading advocate of intervention against Soviet Russia who wanted to 'strangle the Bolshevik baby in its cradle' – unlike Lloyd George, who believed that trade and other contacts would moderate the new regime.

Page 99. Barbusse. Henri Barbusse (1873–1935), an early fellow-traveller with Soviet Communism. Came to fame for his anti-war novels based on his experiences in the First World War. He had just completed his hagiography, *Staline*, when he died in Moscow in 1935.

Page 100. Kalinin. Mikhail Ivanovich Kalinin (1875–1946), token peasant in the Bolshevik leadership. Became nominal President of the USSR under Stalin, who treated him with jovial contempt but let him die a natural death.

Page 101. Budienny. Semyon Mikhailovich Budyenny (1883–1973). The moustachioed former sergeant in the imperial army was one of the victors of the Russian Civil War and rose to the rank of Marshal of the Soviet Union. Performed disastrously during the Second World War when in 1941 he tried to resist the German invaders with the tactics of twenty years earlier. None the less, he survived all his rivals and died loaded with honours under Brezhnev in 1973.

Page 103. Mirbach. Graf Mirbach was the Kaiser's ambassador to the Soviet regime assassinated in Moscow on 6th July 1918 by Left Social Revolutionaries in protest against Lenin's good relations with Imperial Germany. Lenin was severely embarrassed by the incident.

NOTES

Mme Balabanoff. Angelica Balabanov (1869–1965). Born into a wealthy family like so many Russian Marxists, her historical importance lay in her work among Italian Socialists after 1903. She helped to convert many of them to Lenin's faith, which she then rejected in 1921. She failed to influence her former fellow-Marxist, Benito Mussolini, whose Fascist dictatorship forced her out of her adopted Italian homeland. She took revenge on him in her caustic memoirs. After Mussolini's downfall, Balabanov was able to return to Italy, where she died.

Page 114. Asquith. Herbert Henry Asquith, 1st Earl of Oxford (1852–1928). British Prime Minister, 1908–1916. Barrister best known for marrying Margot Tennant, in turn best known for her hats and lovers. Led a reforming government which proved to be the last Liberal majority administration. He turned out to be an ineffectual war leader and was replaced by Lloyd George. Asquith sulked on the opposition benches with a dwindling band of Liberals. In retirement, he returned to his Oxford roots where he failed to win the Chancellorship of the University in 1928 – unlike his most recent biographer, Roy Jenkins, who otherwise remarkably resembles his subject. His only memorable comment was his campaign slogan of 1910, 'Wait and See'. Asquith made his only known witticism – remarking how 'fitting that the unknown Prime Minister should be buried next to the Unknown Soldier' – at the funeral of Lloyd George's short-lived Tory successor, Andrew Bonar Law, the John Major of his day.

Page 127. Louise Bryant – wife of John Reed, later wife of vigorous anti-Communist, William Bullitt.

Page 150. Lunarcharsky. Anatoly Vasiliyevich Lunacharsky (1875–1933), Commissar of Education, 1917–33. Died before Stalin could purge him.